UNDERNEATH
Your Personality

Discover Greater Well-Being
——— Through ———
Deep Living With the Enneagram

Roxanne Howe-Murphy, EdD

Underneath Your Personality
Discover Greater Well-Being Through Deep Living With the Enneagram
Roxanne Howe-Murphy, EdD

Published by Enneagram Press, Santa Fe, New Mexico
Copyright © 2024 Roxanne Howe-Murphy, EdD
All rights reserved.

No part of this publication may be reproduced, stored in a retrieval system, or transmitted in any form or by any means, electronic, mechanical, photocopying, recording, scanning, or otherwise, except as permitted under Section 107 or 108 of the 1976 United States Copyright Act, without the prior written permission of the Publisher. Requests to the Publisher for permission should be addressed to Permissions Department, Enneagram Press or info@roxannehowemurphy.com.

Limit of Liability/Disclaimer of Warranty:
While the publisher and author have used their best efforts in preparing this book, they make no representations or warranties with respect to the accuracy or completeness of the contents of this book and specifically disclaim any implied warranties of merchantability or fitness for a particular purpose. No warranty may be created or extended by sales representatives or written sales materials. The advice and strategies contained herein may not be suitable for your situation. You should consult with a professional where appropriate. Neither the publisher nor the author shall be liable for any loss of profit or any other commercial damages, including but not limited to special, incidental, consequential, or other damages.

Project Management and Book Design: Davis Creative, LLC / CreativePublishingPartners.com
Developmental Editing: Susan Priddy (www.SusanPriddy.com)
Proofreading: Karen L. Tucker (www.CommaQueenEditing.com)

Publisher's Cataloging-in-Publication
(Provided by Cassidy Cataloguing Services, Inc.).

Names:	Howe-Murphy, Roxanne, author.
Title:	Underneath your personality : discover greater well-being through deep living with the enneagram / Roxanne Howe-Murphy, EdD.
Description:	Santa Fe, New Mexico : Enneagram Press, [2024]
Identifiers:	ISBN: 978-0-9793847-7-6 (paperback)	978-0-9793847-8-3 (ebook)	LCCN: 2023915973
Subjects:	LCSH: Enneagram.	Personality.	Presence (Philosophy)	Self-actualization (Psychology)	Well-being.	BISAC: BODY, MIND & SPIRIT / Inspiration & Personal Growth.	SELF-HELP / Spiritual.	PSYCHOLOGY / Personality.
Classification:	LCC: BF698.35.E54 H681 2024	DDC: 155.26--dc23

Roxanne Howe-Murphy
info@roxannehowemurphy.com
www.RoxanneHoweMurphy.com

ADVANCE PRAISE FOR
Underneath Your Personality: Discover Greater Well-Being Through Deep Living with the Enneagram

"This concise book will walk you down a path toward an honest relationship with the multifaceted person you are—the tightly structured chapters and the wisdom within offer a view of an ancient symbol, the Enneagram. The reflections, examples, practices, and key concepts outlined throughout serve as guides for understanding the impact your personality has on how you live your life and on your well-being. The book alone will serve you well, and as a passage to *Deep Living with the Enneagram*, it can serve you as a powerful start towards a life lived with more awareness and more honest connection."

— **Irma Velasquez, DHL, Author,** *Fish Dreams: A Mother's Journey from Curing Her Son's Autism to Loving Him as He Is*, **Artist, Educator, and Social Advocate**

"Embark on a transformative journey with *Underneath Your Personality*. This book serves as a welcoming on-ramp to a more enriched and authentic way of living and offers clarity that makes the complex world of personal growth more easily navigable. What sets this book apart is its seamless integration of the Enneagram, which emerges as a critical ally in the quest for self-understanding. With a gentle yet skillful approach, Roxanne Howe-Murphy offers examples and practical guidance that unveil refreshing insights for novice and experienced explorers alike. Get ready to discover, understand, and liberate the truest version of yourself."

— **Marcia Hyatt, PCC. Author,** *What Have I Mythed? Stories for Reflection*, **Leadership Coach & Creator of** *Best of Ourselves* **Podcast**

"This important book has helped me find grounding, hope, and self-trust in a turbulent time in my life and in the world. It is easy to read, but it takes courage and intention to live by. I appreciate the questions for reflection and the model that clarifies the Enneagram types. Through a daily practice of building the capacity for presence and self-observation suggested in the book, I have reconnected with myself on a deeper level and am more aware of old beliefs and assumptions that no longer serve me. I recommend *Underneath Your Personality* for anyone who feels lost or wants to connect more deeply with themselves and with people around them."

— **Charlotte Heje Haase, Author, Writing/Creativity Mentor, Former Editor of Danish magazine** *Psychology*

"This book possesses the rare ability to liberate the mind and open the heart—a true must-read. With eloquence and simplicity, Roxanne Howe-Murphy skillfully guides the reader through an exploration of human nature, unveiling a clear pathway to kindness, compassion, and a profound, enduring sense of well-being."

— **Diana Redmond, PCC, ICF Mentor Coach, Enneagram Coach and Facilitator, Experiential Learning Leader**

SELECTED PRAISE FOR
Deep Living with the Enneagram: Recovering Your True Nature
Edited and Revised Edition

"Our modern society has trained us to look outside of ourselves for our meaning and fulfillment. We know there is something more—a peace within—and it beckons us. In *Deep Living*, the author identifies that urge for inner connectedness as our soul's call to what is real within—the truth that lies beneath the stories about ourselves. Thankfully, she also shows us how we can navigate the journey back to our essence."

— From the Foreword by **Marci Shimoff**, *New York Times* **Bestselling author**

"One of the greatest discoveries of the past two centuries is that the human personality is not fixed but is flexible, changeable, and malleable. Dr. Roxanne Howe-Murphy is a wise, empathic coach who knows how these changes can be encouraged and facilitated. If you feel stuck in your journey and are ready for growth, change, and greater fulfillment and happiness, let this master coach be your guide."

— **Larry Dossey, M.D., Author,** *ONE MIND: How Our Individual Mind Is Part of a Greater Consciousness and Why It Matters*

"It is a rare book that can bring a reader home to Soul. Roxanne Howe-Murphy's sensitive excavation of the Enneagram awakens the reader to their true human potential. It offers heartfelt, timely guidance from someone who lived every step of what she wrote and who leads her readers back to what we all knew was our task from the very beginning – the embodied, present, and original song of Soul. *Deep Living* is food for the heart, balm for the soul, and light for the spirit."

— **Christina Donnell, Ph.D., Author,** *Encounters with Living Language: Surrendering to the Power of Words, and Transcendent Dreaming: Stepping Into Our Human Potential*

"If you are ready to witness yourself with both eyes wide open, to understand why you act the way you do (even when it is ineffective), and to learn how to live in alignment with your true essence, this is the book for which you have been waiting. Roxanne shares her wisdom, compassion, and deep coaching expertise, leaving you with the gift of **deep living**. A must-read for anyone ready to begin or continue their personal life journey!"

— **Suzanne Glazer, Senior Advisor, Cambridge Family Enterprise Group; Former Assistant Director, Executive Coaching Leadership Initiative, Harvard Business School**

TABLE of CONTENTS

Acknowledgments	1
Introduction	3
CHAPTER ONE Identifying the Disconnect	11
CHAPTER TWO Pursuing Connection	19
CHAPTER THREE Leveraging the Enneagram	35
CHAPTER FOUR Integrating the Power of Presence	89
CHAPTER FIVE Taking the Next Steps	101
Conclusion	111
APPENDIX For Coaches & Human Development Professionals	117
Selected Bibliography	123
About the Author	127
Additional Resources	131
Contact Information	133

Acknowledgments

This book is an outgrowth of colleagues and friends encouraging me to offer an "introduction" to the main principles of my earlier and more expansive books, *Deep Living with the Enneagram* and *Deep Coaching*. I'm especially grateful to the late Nigel Yorwerth, who was my foreign translation and publication rights agent. He spurred me on with a specific request for this version of my work.

Creating this book was almost more challenging than writing the original ones. *Underneath Your Personality* would not have made it to print without the expertise, intuitive insights, enthusiasm, and many masterful contributions of my developmental editor, Susan Priddy. Susan was a dream partner in this endeavor, and she was instrumental in the completion of the project.

The professionals at Davis Creative Publishing Partners have been my production collaborators for years. I greatly appreciate Cathy Davis for helping me navigate the always-changing book world and Missy Asikainen for her design expertise. Their professionalism and dedication are unmatched, and I treasure their friendship. I also want to acknowledge Karen Tucker for bringing her eyes to every detail as a proofreader.

Immense gratitude goes to the dream team at the Deep Living Lab for loving and nurturing the Deep Living approach. I'd like to recognize Irma Velasquez,

Marcia Hyatt, Liz Vanderwerff, Barbara Mathison, Diana Redmond, Jean Blomo, Kerrigan Cross, Laurie Cummins, Pamela Johnson, Samuel Schindler, and Avon Manney. These truly collaborative and brilliant Lab colleagues have individually and collectively supported my work, and they continue to inspire me.

My biggest supporter and most influential, loving companion is my husband, Dr. Jim Murphy. His encouragement and patience naturally became integrated in the pages of this book. No words suffice to express my appreciation for his wise spirit and for being my partner in this life journey.

Introduction

You're running late, and you grab your sunglasses as you head out the door. As soon as you put them on, you realize they're covered in smudges. Everything around you looks a little fuzzy and out of focus. But you don't have time to worry about that right now. You hop in your car and speed off to your appointment.

By the time you arrive at your destination, you've forgotten about the cloudy lenses. Your eyes and your brain have adjusted. You simply got used to the muffled view, even as you unconsciously continue to squint and strain.

Life is often the same way.

Our personalities form the lens through which we see the world. Who we are on the inside colors what we see around us and how we relate to everyone we encounter.

But what if we don't truly know ourselves? What if our view of life is skewed by false assumptions about who we are? What if years of cultural conditioning have smudged our personality lens?

That distorted view creates a level of discomfort lurking just below the surface. And yet, we're busy and distracted, so we learn to live with it. Even as we're unconsciously struggling and straining, we move forward to tackle our to-do lists and go to work and make dinner. Over time, it gets easier to ignore that inner turmoil. In fact, we may start to believe that our muddled view of life must be normal.

It is not.

That's why I'm thrilled to share this book with you. The chapters ahead can help you begin the beautiful journey of cleaning off your cloudy personality lens so you can see yourself and the world around you with clearer vision. That kind of clarity becomes an essential starting point for meeting and accepting the full range of the unique and special person you are.

ABOUT ROXANNE HOWE-MURPHY

- ❖ Master Coach, Coach Educator, and Mentor
- ❖ Teacher, Retreat Leader, and Spiritual Companion
- ❖ Celebrated Thought Leader in Human Transformation and Well-Being
- ❖ #1 International Amazon Best-Selling Author
- ❖ Founder: Deep Living Lab (formerly Deep Living Institute)
- ❖ Founder and Former Faculty: Deep Coaching Institute
- ❖ Former Faculty Member: San Jose State University & Boston University
- ❖ Accredited Teacher: International Enneagram Association
- ❖ Certified Teacher: The Enneagram Institute of New York
- ❖ EdD in Learning & Instruction, Counseling Psychology: University of San Francisco
- ❖ Master's degree in Therapeutic Recreation: San Jose State University
- ❖ Bachelor's degree in Social Work and Sociology: University of Iowa

RoxanneHoweMurphy.com

THE MAIN FOCUS

Consider this: According to scientific research by Harvard Business School professor Gerald Zaltman, around 95% of everything we do, think, believe, and feel takes place below our general level of awareness. What if we're only paying attention to the 5% we consciously notice? That's just the tip of the iceberg! Sadly, we are missing out on the vast majority of who we really area.

One of my passions as a teacher, coach, and writer is to support others in developing their capacities to be at home with themselves through discovering what's been hidden underneath their consciousness. This subject has been an important focus of my career and my life. Starting in 2002, my teaching and writings were fueled by my own "inner work," along with years of study with many wise teachers and colleagues.

In 2008, I built upon that foundation of knowledge to develop a robust method that can transport people from a blurry, peripheral existence to what I call *Deep Living*. This is the process of genuinely understanding who you are as a human being—underneath your personality—so you can increase your well-being and feel comfortable in your own skin.

The term "well-being" is used frequently these days, but did you ever stop to think about what that actually means? While some people interpret it as being physically healthy or having the complete absence of illness, it's much broader than that.

People with maximum well-being have an approach to life that involves understanding and fully accepting who they are emotionally, physically, mentally, and spiritually. They recognize their own gifts, quirks, and shortcomings that are part of being a human, and they embrace those. They know who they are deep down and feel at home with themselves. They possess a sense of connection and wholeness that gives their lives meaning and purpose that would otherwise be missing.

Sounds incredible, doesn't it? ***That's precisely why Deep Living really matters.*** It's designed specifically to boost your well-being. And who wouldn't want more of that?

The first step on the journey toward Deep Living is examining your personality in depth using a profound framework known as the Enneagram. Some people have heard of the Enneagram, and they might think it's just an alternative to other, well-known personality assessments like the Myers-Briggs Type Indicator®. The truth is, the Enneagram is strikingly different and uncovers many more layers of who we are.

I know this from personal experience.

For as long as I can remember, I have been fascinated by the big spiritual questions of life. Who am I, really? And what's my place in this vast, mysterious universe? I spent years doing inner work with the goal of answering those questions. I even changed professions from the world of academia to become a professional coach so I could help others do the same. At the time, I felt like I knew myself well.

It wasn't until I discovered a unique approach to interpreting the Enneagram and began studying its enormous vault of wisdom about the human condition that I realized my relationship with myself was just barely breaking the surface. There was so much more to me than I ever realized!

The Enneagram provided astonishingly accurate reflections about my behavioral, mental, and emotional default patterns. But the most surprising component was its focus on my supposedly secret inner world—the motivations that shaped those patterns. This body of knowledge shined a light on my internal version of who I *thought* I was and showed me I was stuck with a false idea about myself (and about others). Once I recognized that, my journey to make a deeper connection with my true self took a sharp and healing turn. I felt like I had more real choices available to me, and I was taking steps on the road to personal agency and responsibility. Best of all, the insights I gained from the Enneagram gave me an inner freedom that had previously evaded me.

To be clear, the Enneagram wasn't the answer to everything, *but it was the missing piece.* It allowed me to tap into parts of myself I had never known, and the results were life-changing. In fact, my experience with the Enneagram was the catalyst that led me to realize that going beneath the surface of life was a necessary part of feeling more at home with myself.

I do want to stress that Deep Living is much, much more than just analyzing the feedback from a personality assessment. This unique approach involves blending that new level of understanding about ourselves with a heightened sense of awareness and presence. That dynamic combination is the key to elevating our personal well-being and living life to the fullest. You might think of this book as an on-ramp—an introduction to the essential principles for how to do that.

> *"The Enneagram allowed me to tap into parts of myself I had never known, and the results were life-changing."*

THE BENEFITS

There's a miraculous freedom that results from Deep Living and coming face-to-face with yourself, including those parts of you that are underneath your personality and may have been hidden or previously avoided. You might also uncover a precious part of yourself that somehow knows there's more to your life and is silently yearning to be seen. When you bring kindness and compassion to the process of becoming a friend to yourself, you'll discover gratitude and appreciation for the unique being that you are. And as you tap into your deeper realms, your inner sense of well-being will be heightened.

You'll quickly recognize that Deep Living can impact everything you do in a positive way. Every relationship. Every casual interaction with those around you. Every moment you spend alone. Your mental health, your emotional health, your physical health, and your spiritual health. All of it. I've seen people experience radical transformations that started with *really getting to know themselves*. While these changes don't happen overnight, you've already taken a crucial first step on this journey by reading this book.

One of the comments I hear from students and clients who want to know themselves more deeply is, "I have no idea where to look. Where do I begin?" The Deep Living road map you now hold in your hands will provide guideposts for beginning to focus your attention and adopting some important qualities that will help you benefit the most along the way. And if this book speaks to you, there are many Deep Living resources available for support as you continue your inner exploration.

When we unlock the secrets of Deep Living, we can see the world more clearly through the lens of our authentic personality. Fewer smudges and smears. It's my hope that this book will encourage you to embark on a journey of self-exploration that leads to your own experience of Deep Living and results in more confidence, serenity, and harmony in your life.

THE FORMAT

Although it may sound like a paradox, the goal of this book is to provide you with a high-level overview of the Deep Living approach. It's the perfect resource for people who have come to inner work more recently or are new to the idea of Deep Living, as well as those who want a concise foundation for the subject before pursuing more extensive studies.

Besides providing an overview of the Enneagram, this book offers a set of practical tools for everyday use that can help you reorient and discover your truer sense of self. Make no mistake though: This isn't about self-help or self-improvement. It's about unlocking the real mystery of who you are underneath your personality—the complex, wonderful, multifaceted human being that is YOU.

In the pages that follow, we'll discuss these topics:

- Evaluating the negative impact of surface-level living
- Uncovering the reasons behind the unfortunate state of living on autopilot
- Studying the purpose and advantages of connecting with your truer self
- Using the Enneagram as a framework to understand the many facets of your personality—both what's visible and what lies under the surface of your awareness
- Incorporating the practice of presence to feel more at home with yourself

THE JOURNEY BEGINS

I want to express my sincere thanks to you for your interest in Deep Living and for investing the time to read about it. I hope this material will provide inspiration and motivation for you to take the next steps on the very important journey back to yourself, allowing you to integrate the things you learn into your personal and professional life with meaningful results.

Let's get started!

CHAPTER ONE

Identifying the Disconnect

People today are struggling emotionally at higher levels than ever before. In some cases, that pain can be diagnosed as anxiety or depression. For many others, it's a numbness or an inner ache that's much more convenient to ignore.

Do any of these statements sound familiar?

> "If I could just get myself together…"
> "I'm overwhelmed with everything going on in my life. Sometimes I feel empty inside."
> "I spend so much time trying to be the person everyone else wants me to be that I have no idea who I really am."
> "I'm just going through the motions every day. I think I've forgotten what happiness feels like."
> "Why am I even here? Is this all there is?"
> "I feel like I'm the only one who doesn't get it. What's wrong with me?"

If those thoughts resonate with you, you're not alone. It's actually a universal problem—affecting people across the globe, without regard to their socioeconomic status, gender, or backgrounds. There's a widespread epidemic of people experiencing this kind of insidious, just-below-the-surface dissonance. Something inside us doesn't feel quite right, but we can't figure out what it is or how to resolve it. Our lives may be jam-packed with activities, but they seem devoid of meaning.

So, what's behind these underlying struggles? The story that follows will help to address that question.

Imagine you get a big promotion and need to relocate to New York City. The cost of living in Midtown Manhattan is astronomical, so you post on social media to find someone willing to share an apartment. And by apartment, I mean 240 square feet. One bedroom. One bathroom. Extremely close quarters. You sift through the responses, conduct some interviews, and select one of the strangers named Adriana to be your new roommate. The two of you sign a one-year lease.

At the end of that year, you and Adriana have become good friends. You have also gained some fascinating insights about her life.

Adriana is recently divorced and works as a manager for a major retail store. She is a great listener. She tends to juggle a lot of personal and professional projects, so she frequently mentions feeling stressed out. If she picks the movie, it's going to be a comedy. Her grandmother taught her how to make authentic Mexican enchiladas from scratch, and she gets tears in her eyes when she thinks about being in the kitchen many years ago with her sweet *Abuela*. She's definitely a morning person. And she would rather have a root canal than talk about politics or current events.

Recognizing and acknowledging those things about Adriana—her attitudes, behaviors, quirks, and preferences—allowed you to peacefully coexist with her in a tiny apartment for 12 months. **Building a relationship with her was the key to success.**

Now, imagine you have to share an even smaller space with someone, and the lease runs for an entire lifetime. Think that sounds crazy? It's not. Your roommate for every single moment on this planet is…YOU. And the key to success is the same.

> *If you want to live a life that's less stressful and more meaningful, you've got to build a better relationship with yourself.*

That's the answer. When we don't know our true selves, we experience a sense of disconnection that slowly pollutes all the waters of our lives.

RECOGNIZING THE ROADBLOCKS

The task of exploring our inner selves frequently gets overlooked. Some people may not care about it. Others are more focused on getting ahead and being successful in their careers. Some are preoccupied with taking care of others—or worrying about how they're perceived by those around them. The idea of inner reflection rarely crosses their minds, if at all. Or they may just think of it as useless navel-gazing that doesn't change anything.

But what about the people who honestly have at least a passing interest in self-discovery? It's not unusual to initially feel a heavy dose of apprehension when thinking about building a stronger relationship with yourself. How exactly are you supposed to get to know yourself better? What are you really looking for? And what if you don't like what you find? It can be uncomfortable. Maybe even scary.

A great example of that comes from a highly focused man named Justin. He had a well-established career in the field of software development, positioning himself as an expert at creating innovative solutions for the most complex technological problems. The C-suite executives at his company considered him a go-to resource, especially in times of adversity. While he was constantly in high demand, Justin also needed considerable private time to recharge his energy and to stay updated on all the latest industry changes.

Despite the appearance of having an extensive network of contacts, Justin quietly wondered if he had ever actually developed any authentic relationships with all the people around him, even those he cared about. In a safe and private conversation, he admitted that he stays emotionally distanced from others. Taking that a step further, he came to the realization that it feels terrifying to let other people into his private life. He was surrounded by colleagues every day, and yet he was strangely isolated. Justin had resigned himself to believing that's just the way it would always be for him. He felt stuck behind a mental roadblock.

To clarify, some roadblocks on the path to self-discovery are objectively real and difficult, such as not having a stable place to live or not having enough time because of family obligations. But, as with Justin, some roadblocks that feel very real and unyielding are actually a matter of internal perceptions that deserve questioning.

Let's take a look at some of the roadblocks to self-discovery next, recognizing that people often experience interference on several different fronts—both external and internal.

External Distractions

Despite their many benefits, our digital devices bombard us with a nonstop stream of information. Each day, a deluge of text messages, emails, and phone calls boldly compete for our attention. Social media, fueled by the 24-hour news cycle, floods us with constant updates from every corner of the world. Our efforts to feel connected to others can take a serious toll on our connection with ourselves.

Another category of external distractions includes the normal commitments we juggle each day, from our families to our careers to our communities. Our calendars quickly reflect where we put our time and attention. For many people, there are plenty of reasons to neglect inner reflection or rationalize that we simply don't have time.

As if all that isn't enough, the world around us seems to be in constant crisis these days. It can seem almost impossible to focus on ourselves when we're in the midst of economic volatility, political clashes, social unrest, and concerns about climate change: Violence. Discrimination. Wars. Natural disasters. And let's not forget about the lasting impact of a global pandemic. Oh yes, there's a whole lot going on around us!

No wonder we struggle. So many outside forces are coming at us faster than ever, and it's all we can do to keep up. Enhancing a relationship with ourselves may not feel like a priority or even an option.

Internal Interference

Have you ever had a friend who constantly points out your shortcomings and tells you what you are doing wrong? If so, you likely find a way to be busy every time this person wants to get together. Well, the same thing happens inside our own heads.

Meet your Inner Critic. We all have one.

I'm talking about the little internal voice that frequently provides unwanted commentary. Some people manage to ignore it better than others, but it still has a way of stirring up some toxic emotions that create another layer of distraction in our lives.

Perhaps your Inner Critic has bashed you with comments like these:

> "You're such an idiot! Why did you say that? You should have kept your mouth shut."
>
> "You're an imposter. It's only a matter of time before everyone discovers you don't know what you're doing."
>
> "You're not good enough. If you don't try harder and do more, you're going to fail."

Inner Critic messages often lead to a range of negative emotions that can diminish our capacity to lead a fulfilling life. Just like a self-inflicted wound, these harsh comments can result in guilt, shame, anxiety, fear, depression, and loss of personal agency.

Whatever your Inner Critic is whispering in your brain, it likely doesn't make the idea of getting to know yourself better seem very appealing. Remember the annoying friend? "Oh, I appreciate the offer to spend some time working on my inner self today, but I'm really busy. Next week too."

SHARING AN EXAMPLE

I never have to look very far to find an example of the Inner Critic at work. I recently met a woman in one of my workshops who had an idea for an interesting business project she wanted to pursue. She sounded excited about the idea and thought it had a lot of potential. But before she could even take a breath, she started listing all the reasons why she shouldn't move forward.

> "Am I really qualified to take charge of this kind of project? I don't know. What would other people think? Plus, I have so many other tasks I need to take care of first. And what if the whole thing is a complete flop? How embarrassing. On the other hand, what if someone else takes the initiative to lead the project and I get passed over for the promotion?"

Essentially, her Inner Critic was working overtime. It was simultaneously convincing her that she didn't have what it would take to pursue the project while also chiding her for not doing it. It's a safe bet to say she was flooded with the toxic cocktail of negative emotions that the Inner Critic often leaves in its wake: fear and anxiety with an extra shot of shame and guilt.

Bottom line? Our Inner Critics have a real knack for emotional bullying, and they interfere with our ability to look objectively at situations and opportunities. It can be tough for anyone to concentrate and make decisions when they're bombarded with all that negative self-talk.

MOVING FORWARD

No doubt about it, the external distractions and internal interference in our lives can be overwhelming. But there is something we can do to move beyond them. With commitment and intention, we can take steps to reach a sense of wholeness and greater well-being.

The pages ahead describe how to start repairing your emotional disconnect and begin feeling more at home with yourself.

CHAPTER TWO

Pursuing Connection

As you know from the last chapter, substantial roadblocks have a way of keeping people at the surface of life and ignoring what's happening underneath in their hearts, minds, and bodies. Sadly, the disconnect of that outward-facing existence often leaves them feeling separate, incomplete, and unfulfilled. *But there is a compelling path toward greater connection with our inner selves.*

We can make a conscious choice to find out who we are below all the layers of identity we present to the world. And when we do, we'll begin to experience life with more connection and greater contentment. We can reach a point of feeling truly at home with ourselves.

That's what I call **Deep Living**.

THE DEFINITION

Deep Living is based on a strong, grounded, and reliable foundation that integrates ancient wisdom with contemporary scientific and psychological understandings of the human experience. The principles and processes embedded in Deep Living focus our attention on discovering, recovering, and reconnecting with our unique and truer nature so we can learn to live as our authentic selves. It's a journey that we engage in rather than a destination.

What exactly do I mean by "truer nature"?

You may recall from the Introduction that 95% of everything we do, think, believe, and feel takes place below our general level of awareness. Pause for a moment with that statement.

The vast majority of our daily routines are happening on autopilot. We do the same things today that we did yesterday because that's what we've always done. We're creatures of habit.

Hit the snooze button twice. Make the coffee. Let the dog out. Check social media. Complain about the traffic. Go through new emails. Feel irritated by that same coworker who insists on using "Reply All" for every message thread. Try to guess what kind of mood the boss will be in today. Glance at text messages. Consider lunch options. Ponder whether to hit the gym after work.

None of those things are written on a to-do list somewhere. We simply do them or think them or feel them without actually noticing. It's efficient. But the implications of that are absolutely shocking: So much of our lives *just happen*, and we aren't really paying attention.

All of our conscious focus tends to be reserved for the world around us rather than for what's going on inside of us. The unfortunate consequence of this imbalance in focus is that we may not really know who we are below the surface. And whether we acknowledge it or not, that lack of knowing creates inner friction.

On the journey toward Deep Living, we begin to acknowledge and address that underlying friction.

Once we realize there's so much more to us below the surface and allow ourselves to explore that, we can begin to discover what's underneath our thoughts, emotions, and behaviors. In other words, we can be curious about the motivations hidden from our conscious awareness. These motivations might be directly related to the faulty messages we get from the Inner Critic. Here's an example:

> **Inner Critic Message:** "You are responsible for making sure everyone gets along and feels happy. Don't blow it!"
> **Resulting Thought:** "If I express my real opinion on this topic, it will start a huge argument. I don't want to rock the boat, so I won't say anything."

As we gain more awareness and clarity around our hidden sources of interference, we can ask ourselves what is really true about who we are.

> "Hey, wait a minute. Am I really responsible for making sure everyone feels happy? I wonder why I make that assumption… Is that even possible? Besides that, my opinion is valid. Maybe I can learn to share divergent thoughts in a way that sparks interesting conversations instead of arguments. I know that's not how I normally respond, but I think there's an alternative here."

Through Deep Living, we can face what has been driving us (perhaps unconsciously) with kindness and honesty. The process takes us a layer below our usual sense of identity and allows more of our authentic selves to be revealed. That's one of the ultimate goals of Deep Living: to uncover who we really are underneath our personalities and connect it with the person we present to the world.

When our inner and outer selves are consistently in alignment, we'll naturally feel more real with ourselves and more authentic in our interactions with others. In turn, we'll begin to feel more whole, integrated, and fully human. We'll experience greater well-being.

So, how does it work?

In its simplest form, Deep Living involves two basic components that are highlighted in upcoming chapters: 1) using the Enneagram framework to explore deeper aspects of your personality that will likely surprise you; and 2) becoming more intentional about increasing your awareness.

As you expand your awareness, the insights you gain from the Enneagram will begin to create shifts in your attitudes and behaviors that allow you to feel more comfortable in your own skin. The more you uncover, the more alive you begin to feel. That insidious sense of disconnection is replaced by authenticity and the experience of "coming home" to yourself.

Developing a better understanding of your personality also increases your capacity to see yourself more accurately with love and acceptance, quieting the Inner Critic who likes to lash out with negative feedback. I believe there's a boundless freedom in that. We all have our shortcomings and quirks, but we can learn to acknowledge those without feeling compelled to fix each one.

The main thing to remember is that Deep Living can guide you to tenderly build a new relationship with yourself—one that is anchored by self-acceptance and graciousness as well as an objective and nonjudgmental curiosity about who you are.

Imagine what it would be like to trust yourself more.

This orientation does take courage, but I think you'll discover that the healthier relationship you are building with yourself is more than worth it. I realize this approach may contradict how you've typically thought about yourself in the past, especially when it comes to any perceived faults or failings. But don't let the contradiction stop you. I promise you, the power and honesty you encounter through Deep Living will be a welcome shift that could change your future.

THE KEY CONCEPTS

As we continue to unveil the process of Deep Living, several overarching concepts will lead our exploration and lay the groundwork for discussions in the chapters ahead.

Personality

Each one of us has a personality that is part of (but not all of) who we are. If I asked you to describe your personality, you might respond by telling me some of these things:

- ❖ The characteristics you associate with yourself
    (fun, quiet, sensitive, bold, responsible)
- ❖ Your interests, activities, or preferences
    (rock climber, book lover, gardener, musician)
- ❖ Your roles in life
    (spouse, parent, child, neighbor, volunteer, executive, consultant)

These are the dimensions of our personalities that are most obvious and apparent to us. We tend to latch onto those and convince ourselves these external manifestations are the same thing as our inner nature. *(Spoiler alert: They are not.)*

The perception we hold of our personalities can also be unknowingly contoured over time by cultural influences and assumptions. If I'm a health professional, I'm supposed to be caring and sensitive. If I'm a motivational speaker, I'm supposed to be energetic and upbeat. If I'm a corporate leader, I'm supposed to be visionary and strategic. Sometimes our personalities get covered with a shiny coat of expectations that don't necessarily reflect what's happening underneath.

Feedback from other people plays a role in shaping our personalities as well. If my friends give me a hard time about never wanting to pick the movie, I might start to see myself as indecisive. If I get a performance review that questions my productivity, my Inner Critic may tell me I'm a slacker. If I started to believe as a child that I was responsible for taking care of everyone else first and ignoring my own needs, I may forever find myself in the role of caretaker.

The problem with all these personality labels is that they are inherently limiting. We start to live within the narrow walls of who we *think* we're supposed to be—based on our life experiences, our internal neuro-wiring, our career choices, and input from the people around us. Our sense of self can become distorted (either inflated or deflated), and it often doesn't match what is real.

Keeping that in mind, this is the question I'd like to pose to you: **Do you have a grip on your personality, or does it have a grip on you?**

When we're in the grip of our personalities, we may find ourselves inadvertently trapped in a box of artificial identity. If we want to experience life with greater fulfillment, we need to find the courage to open that box and see what's really inside.

As we become more honest and empathetic with ourselves, we can begin to recognize which parts of our personalities are helpful and which ones are no longer effective. By working with the unique perspectives available through Deep Living, we can start to clearly see those differences and identify options that were previously unknown. This new level of awareness can open the door to a practice of gradually letting go of some of our long-held habits.

The results of that change? We start to feel different on the inside. Maybe the shifts we experience are subtle at first, but we may begin to notice that we're growing and responding in new ways as we greet novel circumstances in our lives. We're becoming more flexible, and our personalities are becoming more fluid.

Keep in mind that our personality is not just connected to our thoughts. It's ingrained in every part of our finite nature: in our bodies and the sensations they carry, in our hearts and the range of feelings we habitually experience, and in our busy minds. As you learn more about the Deep Living approach and start with some of its basic practices, what may have felt like separate parts of you will start becoming more connected. And that means you are on the road to feeling more whole.

The big takeaway?

Your personality is a part of you, and it plays a role in how you function in the world. But it's not YOU. If you allow it to completely define you, then you'll continue to feel disconnected and perhaps even suffocate some facets of your inner self that are just waiting to come to life. Working with the principles offered through Deep Living will help you dive underneath your personality and discover a more meaningful way to exist.

Ego Code

Just like our genetic code is a set of rules used by the cells in our bodies, our personalities have their own DNA that I call the *ego code*. In a nutshell, the ego code is a set of invisible rules and inner logic based on our personalities that shapes every aspect of how we experience ourselves. It unconsciously drives the stories we tell ourselves, our choices, our emotional reactions, and our behaviors—for better or worse.

As an example, consider how specific elements of the ego code are involved for these two people deciding whether to take on a new project for a community nonprofit:

> **Nadia:** "There's no way I could volunteer to plan that huge event. I'm a follower, not a leader. No matter what decision I make, people will complain—and that would feel overwhelming. Plus, I'd be so embarrassed if the whole thing was a disaster. Absolutely not."
>
> **Jasmine:** "I don't have time to plan that major event, but everyone will expect me to volunteer as the committee chairperson. I always do. I'm the most organized and creative. I guess it's my responsibility to step up. Again."

Our personalities are directly linked to our emotional reactions, decision-making, and behaviors. But what if the ego code is flawed? Maybe planning a successful event would be just the thing to boost Nadia's confidence. And Jasmine may quickly regret adding yet another project to her already-overflowing plate. If we go along with the false assumptions of our ego codes, we may begin to feel stuck, frustrated, or even resentful.

An essential part of Deep Living is increasing our awareness about our individual ego codes. By being curious about the reasons behind our embedded thoughts, emotions, and behaviors, we may be able to lessen the ego code's potency and impact. That would allow us to go through life with more choices, looking at opportunities through a less rigid lens. In other words, we develop our capacity to broaden our perspectives and try new strategies. The rut that has kept us behaving in certain ways may no longer seem so deep.

Learning to edit the ego code's inner rules and logic can give us the freedom to use new approaches that honor who we are at our core. Here's what that might look like using the previous example:

Nadia: "Yes, I'm an introvert, and I don't feel like I have the energy to take on big projects that involve lots of social interaction. But I do seem to have a way of quietly influencing and engaging the people around me. I don't have to do this all by myself. If I can put together the right team members with a collection of different skills and talents, we could make this event a big success. Plus, I have started to realize that I will be okay even if there are disagreements. They happen within any group, but I've got some strategies to deal with that now."

Jasmine: "If someone asks for volunteers, my hand goes up before my head can process it. But when that happens, I end up feeling exhausted and irritable. I deserve better. From now on, I'm going to pause and remind myself that I don't have to automatically lead every project. I could submit a few creative ideas to the planning committee and then volunteer to help with setup on the day of the event. The party will still be a success, and I won't have to feel frantic inside for the next six months. It's a relief to realize my value isn't tied to being in charge of every project or initiative."

I can tell you this from experience: When people use Deep Living to get curious about the fabric of their ego codes and start untangling the threads, they can move their attention to the inner experience—what's really happening for them below the surface. With that shift, they often have *aha!* moments that upend years of previous beliefs and ideas about their lives. They uncover hidden dynamics that may have been driving their often self-defeating attitudes. Those insights can not only change the way they approach the world, but also generate the healing power of self-compassion for not having realized the root of the problem sooner.

Focus of Attention

One way to begin deciphering the invisible rules of our ego codes is to see what we focus on in our lives. What's getting our time and attention?

The way we organize each day is largely dictated by our personalities. Consciously or unconsciously, we choose the activities and interactions that seem necessary, right, and real to us. Sometimes the faulty wiring of our ego codes can make those choices less than optimal.

For instance, if one of Tyler's personality traits is avoiding conflict, he naturally steers clear of people who are known for controversial statements, boldly diverse opinions, or an argumentative nature. Instead, he focuses his time and attention on people who share his viewpoints—or at least possess a welcoming, open-minded demeanor.

The result of that? Tyler stays in his own safe bubble where no one challenges his status quo, and he inadvertently avoids new ideas and perspectives that could potentially improve his life. His focus of attention becomes stagnant.

For Tyler to break out of this pattern, he could begin noticing his internal experiences. That might involve acknowledging discomfort in his belly when he thinks about dealing with a conflict. He could notice a tightness in his chest when he feels confronted by someone with an opposing viewpoint. Over time, he might recognize his tendency to avoid these uncomfortable sensations, which are known as somatic experiences. (Somatic means "of the body.") That recognition could give him the valuable perspective he needs to eventually address the emotional issues that are triggering his physical symptoms.

Greater awareness could give Tyler a path to expand his focus of attention, uncovering new alternatives and different outcomes.

But when we allow our personalities to drive our focus of attention, we end up with a narrowing field of possibilities. And as time goes by, that becomes more pronounced, defined, and fixed. Anything outside the scope of our increasingly limited emotional vision can create an inaccurate sense of security in our narrow perspectives. We see our solutions as the obvious answer: "This is the way it is." As a result, we may become less understanding of others and more insistent that our way really is the best (or only) way to do something.

In Chapter Five, you'll learn about some basic but potent strategies for working with troublesome or limiting patterns, including the somatic experience.

Core Beliefs

We all have beliefs and values that drive the way we live our lives, even if we can't fully articulate them. Family is the most important thing. God is in charge. Love is all you need. Whatever they are, these beliefs permeate our everyday choices and actions.

But each Enneagram personality type also comes with some specific core beliefs that are connected to the faulty ego code. These type-related beliefs are the central operating principles that shape who we *think* we are and how we respond to life. Unfortunately, the patterns that stem from these inaccurate core beliefs feel like reality to us when, in fact, they are self-limiting habits that perpetuate a myth. They are giving us a false sense of what is actually true.

How does a faulty core belief take up residence within us?

These strongly held assumptions arise unconsciously very early in life, strengthened by difficult experiences or trauma. They take root somewhere deep inside of us and manipulate our view of the world.

Examples of faulty core beliefs might include:

> "Life isn't fair. I always get the short end of the stick."
> "No one really understands me."
> "If I don't win at everything, I'm a loser."
> "I can't trust other people, so I have to take care of myself."
> "If I show any weakness, I'll get hurt."

The problem with core beliefs is that they operate as unconscious filters that only accept supporting information. Regrettably, that means these filters miss and dismiss data that would otherwise provide alternative perspectives. Information that doesn't fit our core belief patterns is subliminally discarded. So, over the years, we might have been exposed to information that could contradict or change that faulty core belief, but we didn't notice it. Or we wrote it off.

Take the man whose core belief involves a lack of trust. He may have trouble forming solid relationships, continually questioning whether a partner will really stay with him. No matter how many times his significant other promises to be there, the words just don't ring true. His core belief still tells him that everyone always leaves eventually. In that way, these inner messages are so loud and powerful that they can become self-fulfilling prophecies.

Bringing awareness, curiosity, and compassion to the journey of discovering our underlying beliefs is what helps to set us free. Deep Living gives us the opportunity to search for the core beliefs that are holding us back, and it opens our minds to information that can prove them wrong.

Core Coping Strategies

Based on our personalities, we each employ certain attitudes and behaviors that help us navigate the inevitable bumps of daily life in the most comfortable manner. The strategies we use are almost automatic, and our responses feel completely natural to us. They make perfect sense in our minds, even when they might not be appropriate in certain instances. We simply develop a go-to reaction for solving problems or dealing with stress, and those actions come with the distinct imprint of our personalities.

Here's an example. Sierra is naturally bubbly and charismatic, and she tends to leverage that energy when facing a challenge. If the restaurant hostess tells her there is a two-hour wait, she smiles and launches into a delightful conversation with hopes she can convince the woman to move her up on the list. The hostess winks and says she'll see what she can do.

In the same situation, James sets out to get a table sooner by leaning into his demanding demeanor. His quick-to-arise anger signals his irritation about the long wait, while pointing out that the call-ahead seating app wasn't working. The hostess is concerned that he might make a scene or ask to speak to her manager, so she discreetly moves him up on the list.

James and Sierra both relied on their personalities as a coping mechanism to deal with a challenge. They fell back on strategies that worked for them many times in the past, even though they might be reinforcing characteristics that lock them into a predictable pattern.

Sierra's natural tendency to smile her way through every problem will fall flat when she needs to have serious conversations with her sister about a family crisis. As for James, his overly confident and slightly aggressive demeanor at the office might lead others to think he is not a good candidate for advancement in a collaborative environment. The patterns can become the problem.

With Deep Living, we can look up close at the core coping strategies we've come to rely on throughout our lives. Even better, we can develop alternatives that may be more effective and give us a broader range of responses when faced with adversity.

Triangles of Identity

To help visualize the components of different personalities in Deep Living, I often use what I call the Triangle of Identity. This image quickly illustrates the elements of an Enneagram personality structure and identifies what's happening below the surface—the parts that we're generally unaware of until they're brought to our attention.

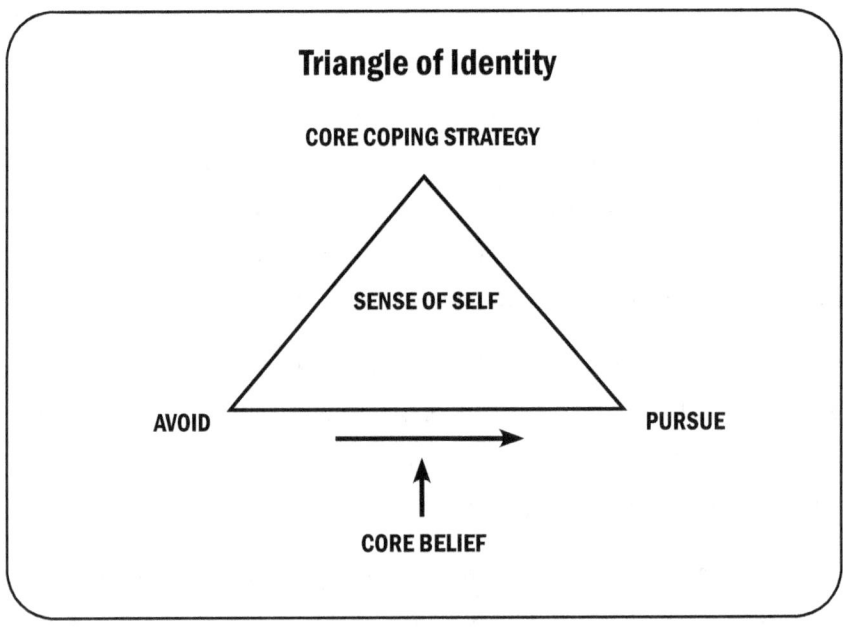

By looking at the Triangle of Identity for a certain Enneagram type, you'll get an at-a-glance view of these elements:

- ❖ What they pursue
    The things they seek, with the assumption that finding them will result in happiness
- ❖ What they avoid
    The things that seem intolerable to them
- ❖ How they cope with stress
    The repetitive behaviors they rely on and the emotional/mental strategies that feel aligned with the way they view themselves
- ❖ How they perceive their own sense of self
    The particular identity they adopt, with little room for expanding beyond the limitations of those self-perceptions

You'll see examples of these Triangles in Chapter Three, and you can get much more information about them in other Deep Living resources. As you read through the examples that follow, you might ask yourself:

- ❖ What am I aware of frequently pursuing in my life?
- ❖ What experience am I aware of wanting to avoid?
- ❖ What strategies am I aware of using to cope when feeling under stress?
- ❖ What internal "sense of self" do I hold without thinking about it?

The Triangles of Identity may help you gain insight into these questions.

THE COMMON THREAD

You may have noticed a similar theme running through each of these key concepts. **Increasing our awareness** is a necessary first step to being more effective in a wider range of circumstances, visualizing more choices, and eventually, feeling more at home with ourselves.

Through Deep Living, we can learn to become more aware of:

- ❖ The personality's drive to maintain control
- ❖ The truer nature that exists underneath the personality
- ❖ The false assumptions driving the inner logic of the ego code
- ❖ The faulty core beliefs that impact the way we see the world
- ❖ The coping strategies that we repeatedly employ, for better or worse

On your quest to experience a deeper sense of the real you, awareness is the mandatory ingredient. You'll find that you are more frequently noticing what's happening inside your mind and your body, underneath the surface—below the "you" that everyone else can see. Think of *noticing* (without judgment) as a capacity you can develop to observe yourself more clearly. *Noticing* allows you to go underneath the stories you've told yourself and into the territory where real change can begin to take place.

I consider this a secret ingredient that opens the doors to developing a new relationship with yourself. As that becomes an integral part of your daily life, one day at a time, you'll begin to connect the dots and fill in some of the gaps you've been experiencing. It has the potential to change everything.

Coming up next, you'll learn more about the primary framework used in the Deep Living process to generate that all-important awareness. Along the way, it will provide you with some fascinating insights as you work to build a stronger relationship with yourself.

CHAPTER THREE

Leveraging the Enneagram

You already know the Enneagram is a pivotal part of the Deep Living approach. But what is it exactly?

The Enneagram is a tried-and-true system for identifying personality types. It can help us dig into who we really are below the 5% of our tip-of-the-iceberg awareness, and it can support remarkable transformation.

We'll start from the beginning.

THE FRAMEWORK

The Enneagram incorporates an enormous field of knowledge and guidance about human behavior and motivation that comes from ancient wisdoms. The basic symbol for the Enneagram was introduced before World War I by philosopher and spiritual teacher G.I. Gurdjieff to highlight the challenges humans experience when they are asleep to their true nature.

Others have advanced this approach through the years, but acclaimed teachers Don Richard Riso and, later, Russ Hudson were among the pioneers who furthered the Enneagram's popularity with their published writings that started in the 1980s. Today, contemporary psychological understanding, spiritual wisdom, and research in the field of neuroscience continue to support the Enneagram's premise.

Through the Enneagram, we learn there are **nine different personality types**. No matter where you live or how old you are, one of these core types will resonate with you more distinctly than others. It may take some time for that to happen, but you will begin to recognize your own personality substantially reflected in one of the nine categories.

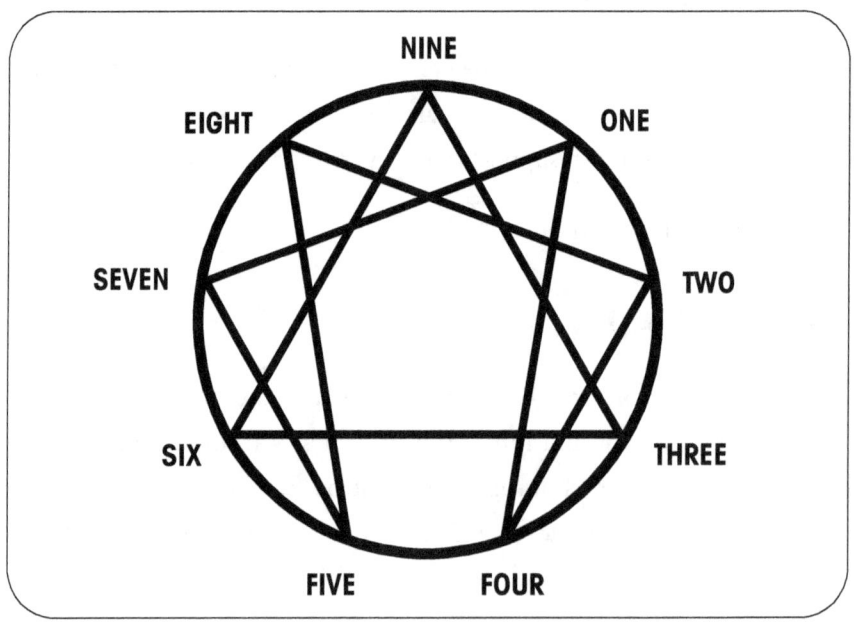

The Enneagram symbol has ancient roots, and each point represents a particular personality type.

Think about what identifying your core type means, especially if you've ever felt like no one else on the planet understands your feelings and perspectives. Your orientation to life—the way you see the world—is shared by about one-ninth of the global population. Stunning concept, isn't it?

It's important to point out that each personality type has inherent value, and none of them are considered good or bad. Just different! Of course, many people can relate to traits in multiple Enneagram types, and one size doesn't fit all. But over the years, the Enneagram endures as a relevant (and shockingly accurate) portrayal of our personalities.

Within this framework, we can take an objective look at our motivations, fears, desires, preferences, attitudes, and the rationale behind our behaviors. It sheds light on our natural tendencies and unconscious habits. Basically, it helps us figure out what makes us tick! Thanks to the Enneagram, we can increase our awareness of *who we believe we are* and what is actually much truer about our nature.

THE ADDED VALUE

Where the Enneagram has an edge over other typing methods is in its ability to indicate whether your natural personality traits are being used in healthy or less-than-healthy ways. Within each personality type, the Enneagram identifies a **full continuum of presence**, according to Riso and Hudson. That is, the less we are in the grip of our personalities, the more present we are able to be. The opposite is also true: The more we identify with our personality traits, the less present we are. This is a humbling awareness.

These additional layers of insight enable you to look at the variation in the core elements of your personality—like why you might show up so differently within the space of a few minutes. You could be humming along, feeling happy, until you find yourself in a rage over a noisy neighbor on an otherwise-quiet morning. The Enneagram can provide you with a powerful understanding of your own range of feelings and behaviors, as well as some of the underlying factors that feed into your experiences.

These more precise findings available through the Enneagram are not easily captured through other assessment methods, and they are an essential ingredient for the process of Deep Living.

Here's an example. Danita worked as an executive assistant in a large corporation. She was very good at her job, but she'd be the first one to tell you that the purpose of her weekday income was to fund the real passions she pursued on the weekends: playing her guitar in an all-girl folk band and selling her watercolor paintings at regional art festivals.

Danita exuded creativity in everything she did—from her words and actions to the way she dressed. Her clothing and makeup were often whimsical. Some days she arrived at the office with her waist-long brown hair braided with colorful wildflowers. Other days, her hair was piled on top of her head in a towering bun that made her look like she might tip over. Her coworkers seemed to get a kick out of her quirky nature, and she took it as badge of honor when they referred to her as "the crazy one." Being original was her signature feature.

When Danita's company was purchased by a much larger organization, the new leadership team was less enthused about her distinct appearance. They wanted everyone to present a more formal, professional image for any potential clients who might be visiting the offices. Danita assured the new director that her eccentric nature was actually an advantage. "The clients love it. They always come by to say hello and see what wacky thing I'm wearing," she exclaimed. "I mean, this is who I am. Why would you want me to look like a cookie-cutter version of every other person in here? That's boring!"

When the director insisted she adopt a more corporate look, Danita begrudgingly made some changes. She went along with the guidelines (for the most part), but she made sure everyone knew she wasn't happy about it. She showed up to work every day with a decidedly sour mood, and her coworkers started to keep their distance. A caring colleague finally pulled her aside and told her she might be a target during the upcoming layoffs if she didn't "chill out" a bit.

Danita's frustration was at a boiling point. She needed the income from that job and had many friends in the office, but she just couldn't seem to get past the absurd restrictions on her personal style.

The next Saturday, Danita shared her situation with a friend named Rakesh from one of her art festivals. He could see the frustration in her eyes. "I know I should just get over it and fall in line, but I can't. I don't know why. I just can't."

Rakesh smiled and gave her a hug. Then he asked her if she had ever heard about using the Enneagram to learn more about her personality. As he told her more, she was both curious and skeptical. She didn't like the idea of being "put into a box" that narrowly defined who she was. She was proud to be complex and multilayered. However, with Rakesh's support, she was willing to move forward and find out more.

Upon discovering her Enneagram type, Danita realized that her quest for originality was a part of her nature. Her response to being toned down was perfectly normal for her; there wasn't anything wrong. But she also saw how that characteristic was working against her at the office.

Once she realized the impact she was having on the people around her, she began to get curious about what motivated her approach to life. With greater awareness and understanding about why she was holding onto faulty beliefs about herself (along with a bit more humility), she was able to funnel her originality and emotional intensity into her art and music. Danita found a way to be her authentic self while also accommodating the "rules of play" with the new leadership team. More importantly, she began to feel at peace with that balance.

We can also witness a spectrum of emotions in the life of a man named Harris. He found himself bewildered by his relationships with some of his family members.

Harris was well-liked at work and excelled at facilitating the resolution of thorny situations in a nonprofit organization specializing in community mediation. But somehow, his strong people skills were not effective on the home front. His teenage offspring chafed against what they considered his constant intrusion on their lives, while Harris just saw his behavior as expressing his interest and love for them. He often felt underappreciated for his efforts.

Once Harris became aware of his core Enneagram type, he began to recognize that he could be overbearing and unfairly demanding of his teenagers' time. He was surprised and a bit embarrassed when he realized the unexpected impact he had been having on his family. He gained a better understanding of his own needs and learned to visualize how his natural personality traits could be expressed in a continuum of healthy to less-than-healthy ways.

As you can see, the true brilliance of the Enneagram is found in this dual system of feedback. It allows us to see the gifts of our personalities as well as the surprising ways in which we are unconsciously creating our own roadblocks. That combination gives us a unique window for looking beyond the surface of our behaviors and emotions to see what lies underneath them. That's where the real inner work takes place.

THE PERSONALITY TYPES

As you move toward the intention of Deep Living, the Enneagram can fill in many of the missing pieces and accelerate your journey. For the purposes of this book, I am providing a concise summary of each Enneagram type to demonstrate the different variations on how people "do life." However, there are many resources available that provide more extensive examples and case studies for each personality type. A number of those are cited at the end of this book.

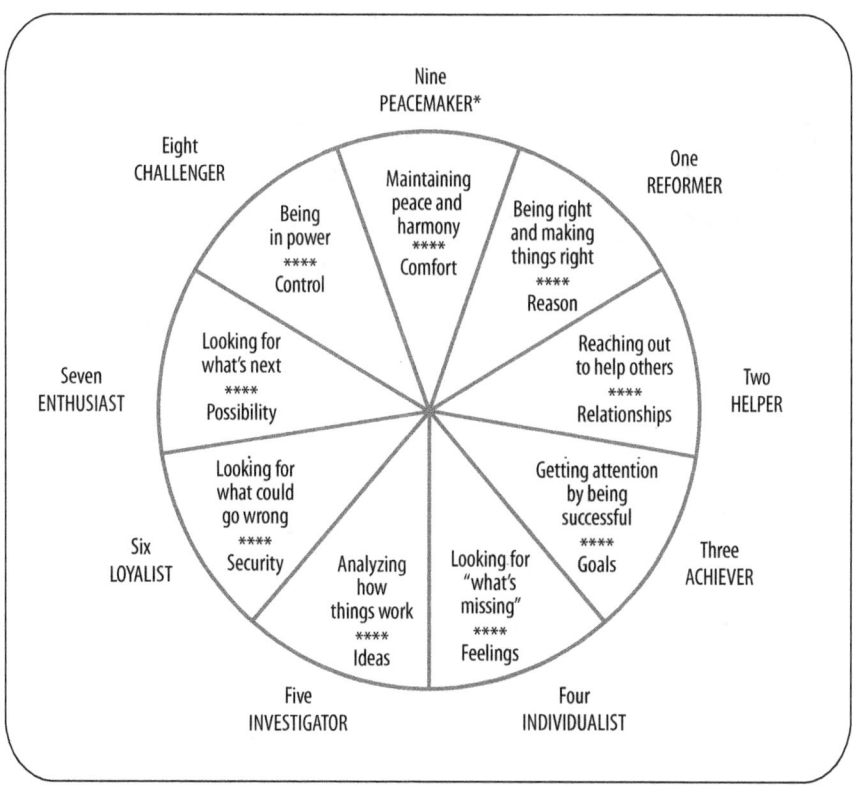

The names of the Enneagram types are those of Riso and Hudson.

This illustration provides a high-level overview of the nine Enneagram personality types and a quick glimpse at the focus that drives each one.

Read through the Enneagram profiles that follow and take some time to reflect on each one. You'll find a few questions to consider at the end of the sections, along with space to jot down your notes.

I do feel compelled to add an important comment here. Be careful about automatically assuming you know your Enneagram type by reading these brief descriptions. Our perceptions about *who we think we are* can sometimes skew the truth. Remember, two people with the same Enneagram type can behave very differently if they are operating at different points on the more-to less-healthy spectrum. It's not a cut-and-dried evaluation. I'm a prime example of that since my original guess at my own Enneagram type was close but inaccurate.

Keep an open mind as you read, and resist the urge to claim one type before you've explored all the options. I encourage you to take a few breaths and feel your feet on the floor as you begin to examine these personality profiles.

Enneagram at a Glance

TYPE 1: THE REFORMER

PROFILE

Gifts & Healthy Traits:	Principled, purpose-driven, conscientious, wise.
Sense of Self:	I am reasonable, objective, and responsible.
Focus of Attention:	Doing things right and being right.
Pursues:	Being right and doing good.
Avoids:	Being wrong or bad.
Faulty Core Belief:	I can't afford to make a mistake, so I always need to be careful.
Core Coping Strategy:	Being on a mission.
Inner Critic Message:	If I don't do what's right, I'm not good.
Less Healthy Traits:	Opinionated, judgmental, perfectionistic, self-critical.

COMMON EXPERIENCES
Thoughts, Feelings, and Physical Sensations

▲ HEALTHIER

- ❖ I have a strong inner compass for what is morally right and wrong.
- ❖ I have high standards for myself and all the people around me.
- ❖ It's my responsibility to do things correctly, and I'll work tirelessly to make that happen.
- ❖ The means and the ends are equally important, and I'd never sacrifice one for the other.
- ❖ I have a lot of opinions, and I'm not afraid to express them.
- ❖ I feel obligated to be perfect, so I spend a lot of energy trying not to make mistakes.
- ❖ I work to control myself and push away any frivolous impulses.
- ❖ I carry a lot of tension in my neck and shoulders.
- ❖ Feelings are irrational and messy. I just suppress them.
- ❖ I am constantly critical of myself, and sometimes that spills onto others.
- ❖ I don't mean to sound condescending, but I'm confident I know the right way to do things. Let me show you how.
- ❖ Nothing is worse than being criticized and told something is my fault.

▼ LESS HEALTHY

TRIANGLE OF IDENTITY

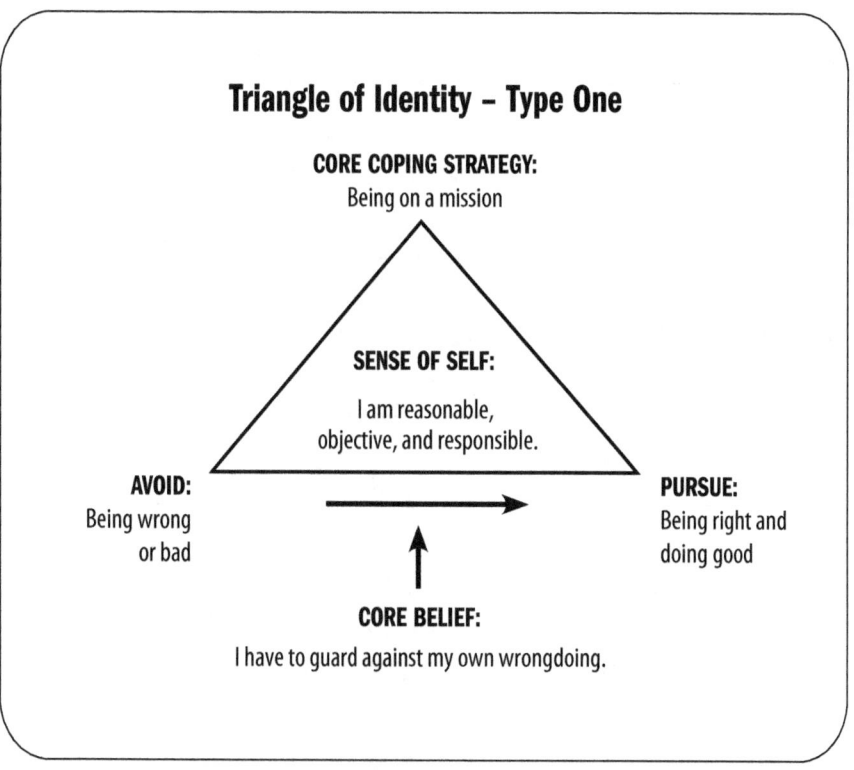

REFLECTION

Do these descriptions resonate with you? If so, how?

_____

_____

_____

If not, do they sound like someone you know?

_____

_____

_____

What questions do you have about this personality type?

_____

_____

_____

What's the main takeaway for you?

_____

_____

_____

Enneagram at a Glance

TYPE 2: THE HELPER

PROFILE

Gifts & Healthy Traits:	Empathetic, nurturing, openhearted, warm, generous.
Sense of Self:	I am loving, caring, and selfless.
Focus of Attention:	Building relationships and doing things for others.
Pursues:	The experience of love.
Avoids:	Being seen as selfish.
Faulty Core Belief:	The needs of others must come first.
Core Coping Strategy:	Serve and support others to get their love and appreciation.
Inner Critic Message:	If I'm not loved and accepted by others, I'm not good.
Less Healthy Traits:	People-pleasing, enabling, possessive, martyr-like, resentful.

COMMON EXPERIENCES
Thoughts, Feelings, and Physical Sensations

▲ HEALTHIER

- ❖ I am open-hearted and loving without conditions.
- ❖ I enjoy being generous to others and to myself.
- ❖ I am proactive about recognizing and meeting the needs of other people.
- ❖ I invest time and energy giving to others to create real connections with them.
- ❖ When I selflessly care for others, they will love and accept me.
- ❖ It would be selfish to think about my own needs.
- ❖ I sometimes feel guilty for not doing more to support other people.
- ❖ I can wear myself out when I focus more about others than I do myself.
- ❖ It's hard for me to say no, and I think people sometimes take advantage of that.
- ❖ I feel uncomfortable asking others for help. That's supposed to be my role.
- ❖ My stress can build when I feel obligated to take care of too many people or things.
- ❖ I sometimes resent those I help if they don't appreciate me enough.

▼ LESS HEALTHY

TRIANGLE OF IDENTITY

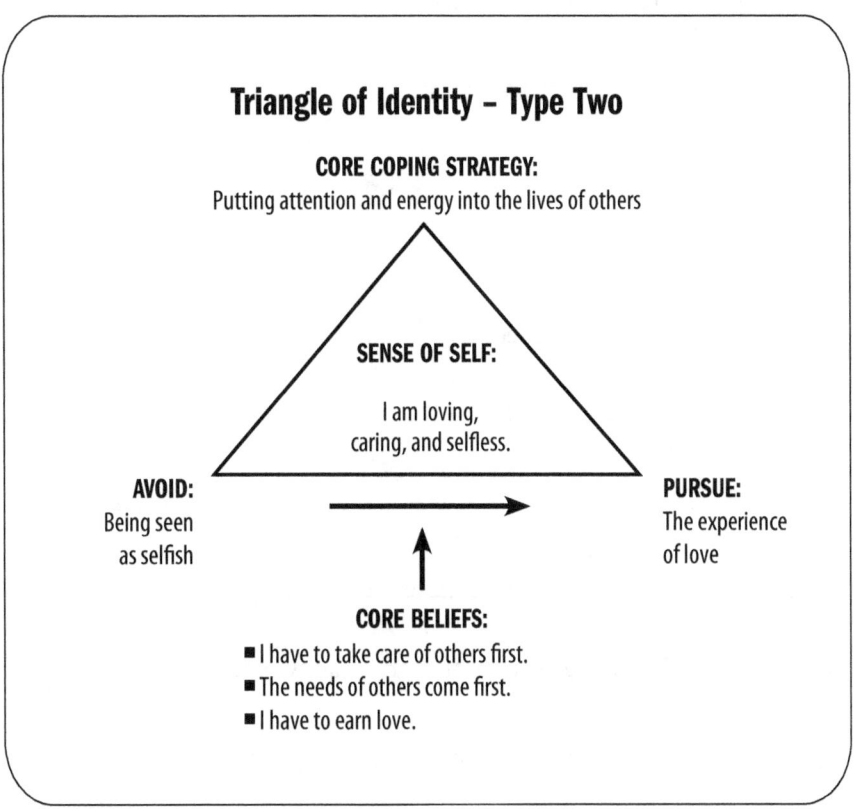

REFLECTION

Do these descriptions resonate with you? If so, how?

___

___

___

If not, do they sound like someone you know?

___

___

___

What questions do you have about this personality type?

___

___

___

What's the main takeaway for you?

___

___

___

Enneagram at a Glance

TYPE 3: THE ACHIEVER

PROFILE

Gifts & Healthy Traits:	Growth-oriented, confident, ambitious, flexible, inspiring.
Sense of Self:	I am accomplished and driven with unlimited potential.
Focus of Attention:	Getting noticed for my achievements and success.
Pursues:	Being seen as having value.
Avoids:	Being seen as a failure.
Faulty Core Belief:	My worth and my value come from my accomplishments.
Core Coping Strategy:	Perform, adapt, and push to be the best.
Inner Critic Message:	If others don't think I'm successful, I'm not good.
Less Healthy Traits:	Overly competitive, excessively image/status conscious, guarded, self-promoting.

COMMON EXPERIENCES
Thoughts, Feelings, and Physical Sensations

HEALTHIER ▶

- ❖ I want to contribute and achieve things that make the world a better place.
- ❖ I'm a good role model, and I excel at motivating and inspiring others.
- ❖ I quickly adapt and produce results, no matter what environment I'm in.
- ❖ I set goals and do whatever it takes to be the best. Second place is not acceptable.
- ❖ I avoid putting myself in situations where I might not succeed.
- ❖ I thrive on being recognized for my accomplishments, but the "high" never lasts.
- ❖ I can be emotionally guarded so other people won't see that I'm feeling insecure.
- ❖ Appearances matter, and I am highly sensitive to the image I project to others.
- ❖ Sometimes I feel like I'm performing during interactions with others, and I feel the pressure to always be "on."
- ❖ I put on the mask of a certain persona that matches what I think others expect from me.
- ❖ I want people to think well of me, and sometimes that leads me to stretch the truth.
- ❖ Dealing with failure is the hardest thing in life for me.

▼ LESS HEALTHY

TRIANGLE OF IDENTITY

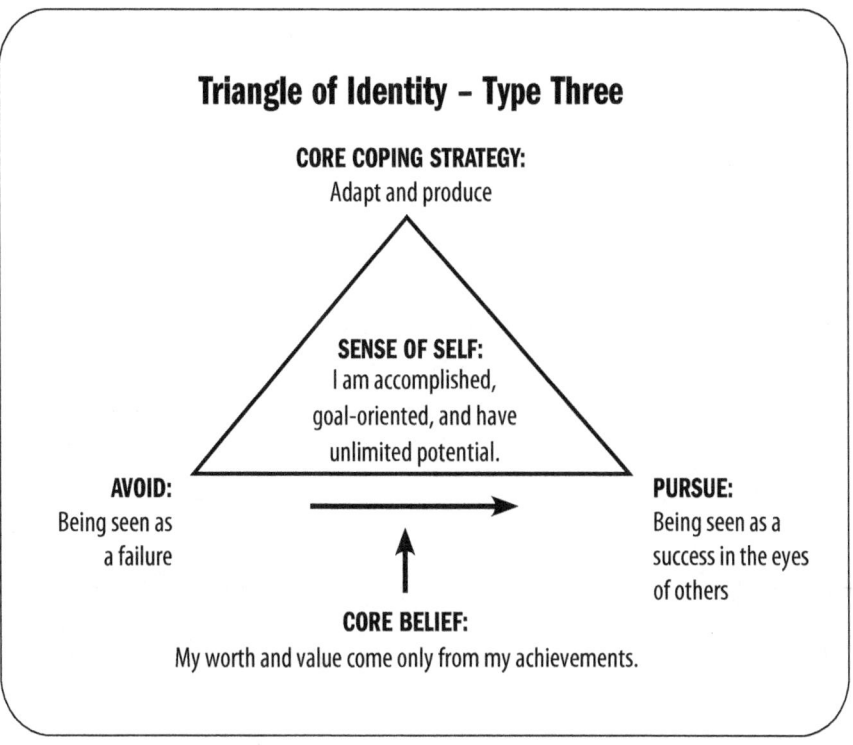

REFLECTION

Do these descriptions resonate with you? If so, how?

_____

_____

_____

If not, do they sound like someone you know?

_____

_____

_____

What questions do you have about this personality type?

_____

_____

_____

What's the main takeaway for you?

_____

_____

_____

Enneagram at a Glance
TYPE 4: THE INDIVIDUALIST
PROFILE

Gifts & Healthy Traits:	Emotionally intelligent, creative, honest, expressive, engaged.
Sense of Self:	I am unique, intuitive, and sensitive.
Focus of Attention:	Being original and searching for who I really am.
Pursues:	Finding out who I am.
Avoids:	Being ordinary.
Faulty Core Belief:	I am missing something important.
Core Coping Strategy:	Create emotional intensity.
Inner Critic Message:	If I'm not true to myself, I'm not good.
Less Healthy Traits:	Moody, envious, self-absorbed, overly dramatic, temperamental.

COMMON EXPERIENCES
Thoughts, Feelings, and Physical Sensations

◄ HEALTHIER ▲
▼ LESS HEALTHY

- ❖ I am engaged in life, and I feel solidly connected and present with others.

- ❖ I am aware of my emotions and sensitive to the emotions of other people.

- ❖ I know how to make other people feel deeply seen and understood.

- ❖ Other people are often inspired by the depth of my creativity, authentic expression, and originality.

- ❖ I'm not afraid to ask difficult questions or be with people in painful situations.

- ❖ Emotions are the truth and the basis for life. I feel compelled to follow them wherever they lead.

- ❖ I can generate intense feelings through my imagination, often fantasizing about what my life should be.

- ❖ The usual rules of life don't apply to me.

- ❖ I can be dramatic, and some might consider me high maintenance.

- ❖ Sometimes I feel misunderstood and alone. I just wish someone would rescue me.

- ❖ People may walk on eggshells around me because they don't know what mood I'll be in.

- ❖ I feel like something is missing in myself, and that can make me envious of others.

TRIANGLE OF IDENTITY

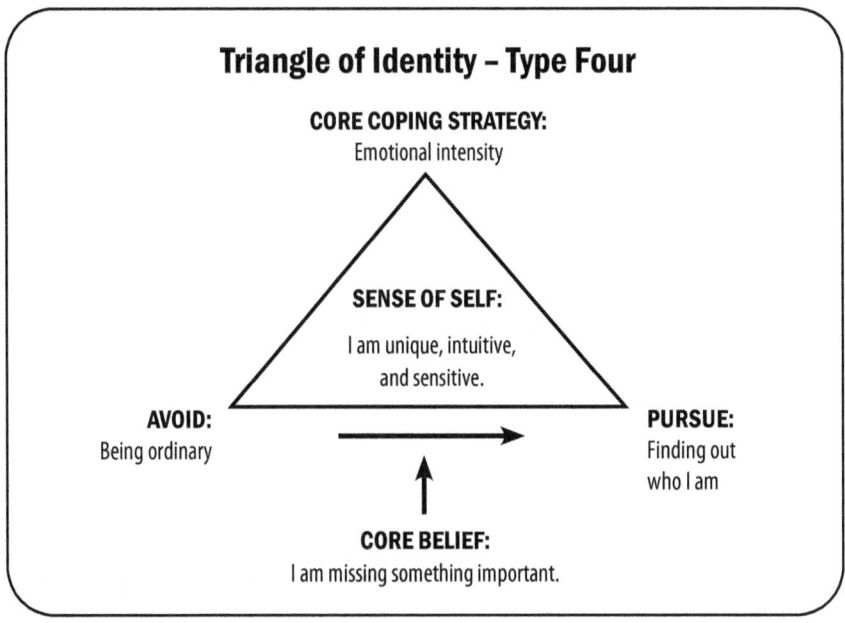

REFLECTION

Do these descriptions resonate with you? If so, how?

_____

_____

_____

If not, do they sound like someone you know?

_____

_____

_____

What questions do you have about this personality type?

_____

_____

_____

What's the main takeaway for you?

_____

_____

_____

Enneagram at a Glance

TYPE 5: THE INVESTIGATOR

PROFILE

Gifts & Healthy Traits:	Curious, focused, insightful, pioneering, self-sufficient.
Sense of Self:	I am smart, perceptive, and observant.
Focus of Attention:	Understanding how things work and solving problems.
Pursues:	Knowledge, understanding, making a contribution.
Avoids:	Being ignorant.
Faulty Core Belief:	I'm on my own, so I have to figure it out for myself.
Core Coping Strategy:	Apply mental intensity.
Inner Critic Message:	If I don't master something, I'm not good.
Less Healthy Traits:	Arrogant, private, emotionally detached, secretive, agitating.

COMMON EXPERIENCES
Thoughts, Feelings, and Physical Sensations

▲ HEALTHIER

- ❖ I am insatiably curious, and I love to learn new things about how the world works.
- ❖ I have the capacity to be a trailblazer who introduces new ideas and finds breakthrough solutions.
- ❖ I can see things with a clear, objective mind without letting emotions get in the way.
- ❖ People appreciate my wonderment about life and my clever wit.
- ❖ I am a private person, and I like to work by myself without interruptions.
- ❖ I feel compelled to know everything possible about selected, often rare, subjects.
- ❖ I often observe rather than participate in life.
- ❖ I need to be well prepared before taking action, and I don't like to be rushed.
- ❖ I tend to live in my own mind, where I analyze all the data I've gathered.
- ❖ I sometimes push people away when I feel overwhelmed by their emotions, life situations, and needs.
- ❖ Some people may perceive me as intellectually arrogant.
- ❖ My propensity to withdraw from others can sometimes take me to a dark place, which leads me to provoke or agitate the people around me.

▼ LESS HEALTHY

TRIANGLE OF IDENTITY

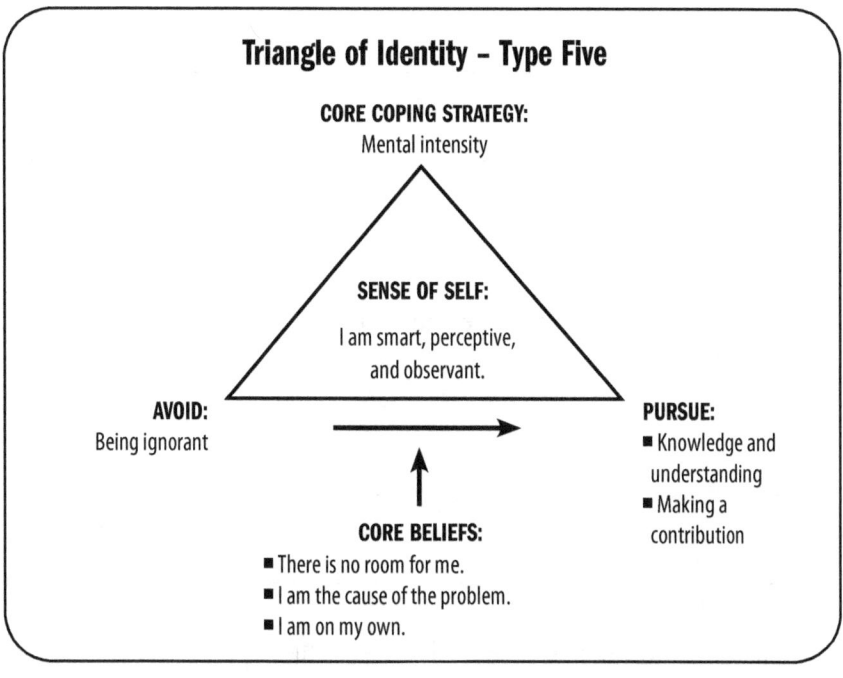

REFLECTION

Do these descriptions resonate with you? If so, how?

_____

_____

_____

If not, do they sound like someone you know?

_____

_____

_____

What questions do you have about this personality type?

_____

_____

_____

What's the main takeaway for you?

_____

_____

_____

Enneagram at a Glance

TYPE 6: THE LOYALIST

PROFILE

Gifts & Healthy Traits:	Trustworthy, cooperative, committed, open, aware.
Sense of Self:	I am responsible, reliable, and vigilant.
Focus of Attention:	Preparing for what might go wrong to keep myself and others safe.
Pursues:	Security and something to hold onto.
Avoids:	The unfamiliar or the unknown.
Faulty Core Belief:	The world is threatening and dangerous; I can't trust others.
Core Coping Strategy:	Look for something I can trust.
Inner Critic Message:	If I don't know what's expected of me, I'm not good.
Less Healthy Traits:	Suspicious, doubtful, anxious, pessimistic, indecisive.

COMMON EXPERIENCES
Thoughts, Feelings, and Physical Sensations

▲ HEALTHIER

- ❖ Trusting my own guidance, I also make others feel included and valued.
- ❖ I am cooperative, and I see others as equal contributors to efforts that benefit all.
- ❖ Other people appreciate my trustworthiness and my stewardship toward issues I care about.
- ❖ I take my commitments seriously and always follow through. People can count on me.
- ❖ I put a lot of energy into creating plans and systems that create safety and security.
- ❖ I like to know exactly what is expected of me so I can fulfill my obligations. Not knowing makes me nervous.
- ❖ I tend to think about all the things that could go wrong, and sometimes the worry paralyzes me.
- ❖ I am often suspicious of authority and unsure about whom I can trust.
- ❖ I feel stress when I am overcommitted or faced with unfamiliar situations.
- ❖ I can become overwhelmed by doubt and anxiety, which may give me a pessimistic outlook and render me unable to make decisions.
- ❖ Sometimes I avoid the pain of second-guessing myself by being pushy and taking action without any thought.
- ❖ I tend to magnify the negative possibilities and outcomes, seeing normal adversity as catastrophic.

▼ LESS HEALTHY

TRIANGLE OF IDENTITY

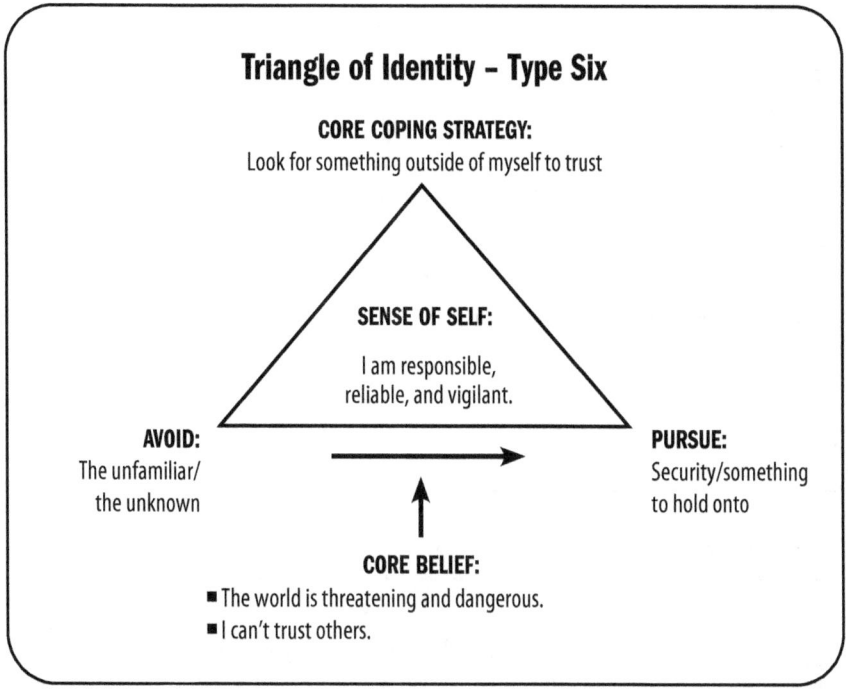

REFLECTION

Do these descriptions resonate with you? If so, how?

_____

_____

_____

If not, do they sound like someone you know?

_____

_____

_____

What questions do you have about this personality type?

_____

_____

_____

What's the main takeaway for you?

_____

_____

_____

Enneagram at a Glance

TYPE 7: THE ENTHUSIAST

PROFILE

Gifts & Healthy Traits:	Playful, versatile, quick-minded, joyful, entertaining.
Sense of Self:	I am free, spontaneous, fun, and full of life.
Focus of Attention:	Exploring a world full of possibilities.
Pursues:	Open-ended freedom to find happiness.
Avoids:	Being caged in.
Faulty Core Belief:	My source of satisfaction comes from outside of me.
Core Coping Strategy:	Stay alert so I don't miss out on something.
Inner Critic Message:	If I don't get what I need, I'm not good.
Less Healthy Traits:	Scattered, distracted, uninhibited, excessive, perpetually dissatisfied.

COMMON EXPERIENCES
Thoughts, Feelings, and Physical Sensations

HEALTHIER ▲

- ❖ I am a truly joyful person. I'm in love with life, and I'm extraordinarily grateful for it.
- ❖ I have an adventurous spirit, and I want to experience everything the world has to offer.
- ❖ My enthusiasm invigorates the people around me.
- ❖ Others find me entertaining, and they enjoy my humor, wit, and sense of fun.
- ❖ I love to meet new people, try new gadgets, and participate in new experiences.
- ❖ I move to where the grass is greener, and it always seems to be greener somewhere else.
- ❖ I spend a lot of time focusing on what's next instead of experiencing what's happening now.
- ❖ My nonstop energy can be scattered and unfocused, making it hard to stay on task or complete projects.
- ❖ I like to keep my options open, waiting to make plans until the last minute in case something better comes along.
- ❖ I get bored easily, and I often feel restless.
- ❖ I get frustrated when I can't do what I want and pursue the instant gratification I need.
- ❖ I am uninhibited and don't feel the need to limit myself.

▼ LESS HEALTHY

TRIANGLE OF IDENTITY

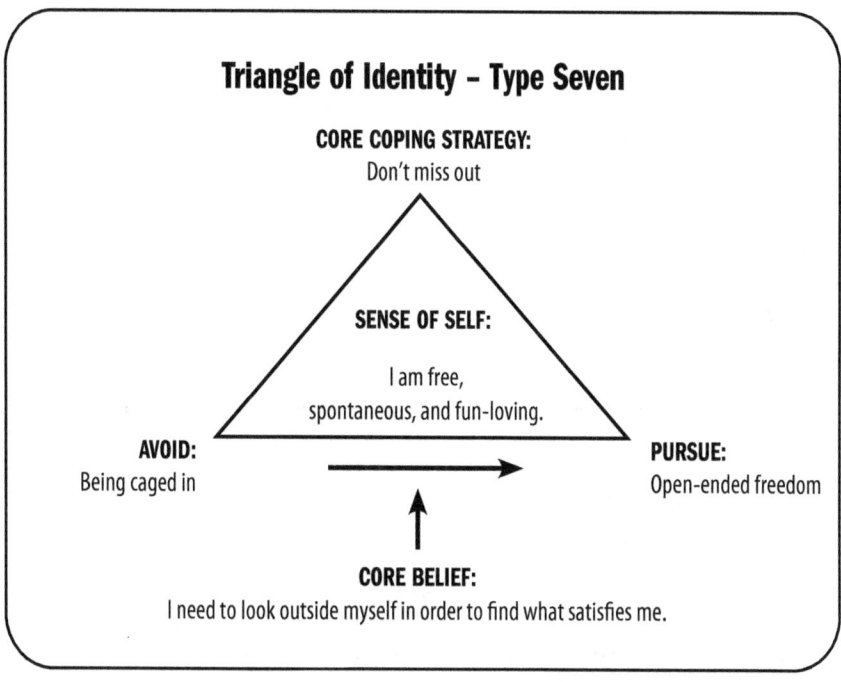

REFLECTION

Do these descriptions resonate with you? If so, how?

_____

_____

_____

If not, do they sound like someone you know?

_____

_____

_____

What questions do you have about this personality type?

_____

_____

_____

What's the main takeaway for you?

_____

_____

_____

Enneagram at a Glance

TYPE 8: THE CHALLENGER

PROFILE

Gifts & Healthy Traits:	Visionary, assertive, decisive, courageous, charitable.
Sense of Self:	I am strong, in control, and self-reliant.
Focus of Attention:	Being powerful and in control of my territory.
Pursues:	Feeling powerful.
Avoids:	Being vulnerable.
Faulty Core Belief:	It's a hard, unjust world. It's not safe to be soft or vulnerable.
Core Coping Strategy:	Take charge.
Inner Critic Message:	If I can't get my own way and impose my will, I'm not good.
Less Healthy Traits:	Confrontational, intimidating, insensitive, domineering, intense.

COMMON EXPERIENCES
Thoughts, Feelings, and Physical Sensations

HEALTHIER ▲

- ❖ I'm passionate about causes I believe in, and I have a big heart for supporting them.
- ❖ I have the confidence and courage to get things done and overcome obstacles.
- ❖ I can inspire other people with my generosity of spirit and my capacity to take a stand.
- ❖ I respond quickly to problems by advancing appropriate solutions—ones that are obvious to me but not always to others.
- ❖ I am direct and straight to the point. I call it like I see it.
- ❖ I like the intensity of playing high stakes, and sometimes I take big risks.
- ❖ I like to exert my stature, influence, and power.
- ❖ I don't like to compromise.
- ❖ I'm not always sensitive to others, which can leave them feeling unheard, unseen, and unappreciated.
- ❖ I talk big and make bold promises that I often cannot keep.
- ❖ I like to take charge, but my intensity can sometimes be experienced as confrontational and domineering.
- ❖ When people threaten my control, I may express that fear as rage and anger.

▼ LESS HEALTHY

TRIANGLE OF IDENTITY

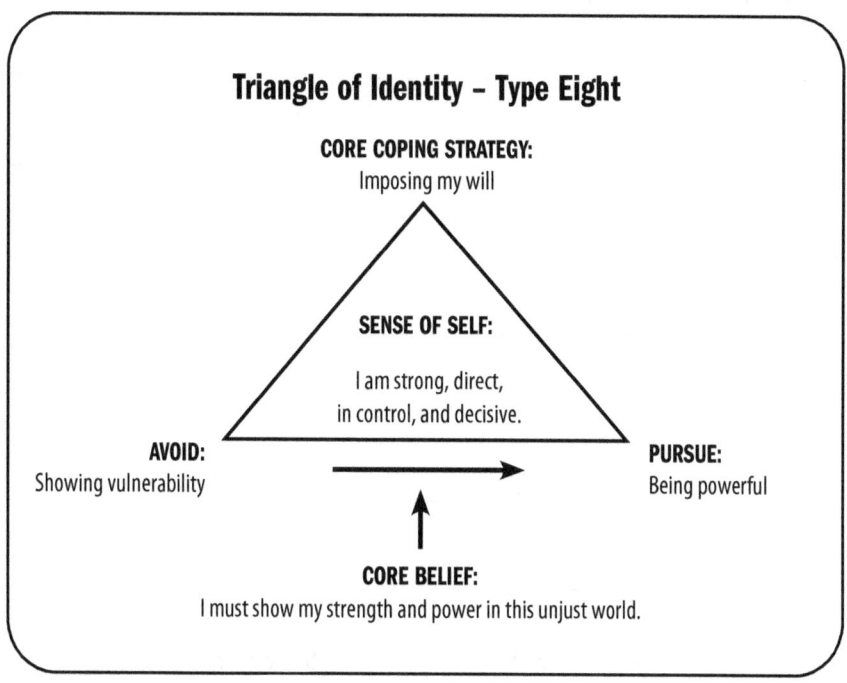

REFLECTION

Do these descriptions resonate with you? If so, how?

_____

_____

_____

If not, do they sound like someone you know?

_____

_____

_____

What questions do you have about this personality type?

_____

_____

_____

What's the main takeaway for you?

_____

_____

_____

Enneagram at a Glance

TYPE 9: THE PEACEMAKER

PROFILE

Gifts & Healthy Traits:	Receptive, accepting, patient, unpretentious.
Sense of Self:	I am calm, peaceful, and easygoing.
Focus of Attention:	Creating peace and harmony.
Pursues:	Comfort and interconnectedness.
Avoids:	Severing of connection.
Faulty Core Belief:	I don't matter. I need to erase myself to stay connected to others.
Core Coping Strategy:	Accommodate others and avoid being noticed.
Inner Critic Message:	If everyone around me isn't okay, I'm not good.
Less Healthy Traits:	Stubborn, apathetic, repressed, numb, ruminating.

COMMON EXPERIENCES
Thoughts, Feelings, and Physical Sensations

HEALTHIER ▲

- ❖ I remember my priorities and am self-determining.
- ❖ I am able to accept others as they are and where they are.
- ❖ I am unpretentious. What you see is what you get. I'm genuine.
- ❖ I recognize the potential in other people and see what's possible for them.
- ❖ I am a bridge builder. I'm good at listening to others, understanding their differences, and finding ways to bring people together.
- ❖ It feels natural to me to make others feel loved, accepted, and valued.
- ❖ I tend to be self-effacing and downplay my contributions to avoid the spotlight.
- ❖ It's easier to go along with others and their agendas so I don't create any conflict.
- ❖ I sweep my own ideas and agendas under the rug so I don't risk ruining any relationships.
- ❖ I often operate on autopilot and withdraw if situations become emotionally uncomfortable.
- ❖ I avoid conflict like the plague, so I may appear apathetic or indifferent to others.
- ❖ I sometimes leave people feeling confused by my outward niceness and my inner stubbornness.

▼ LESS HEALTHY

TRIANGLE OF IDENTITY

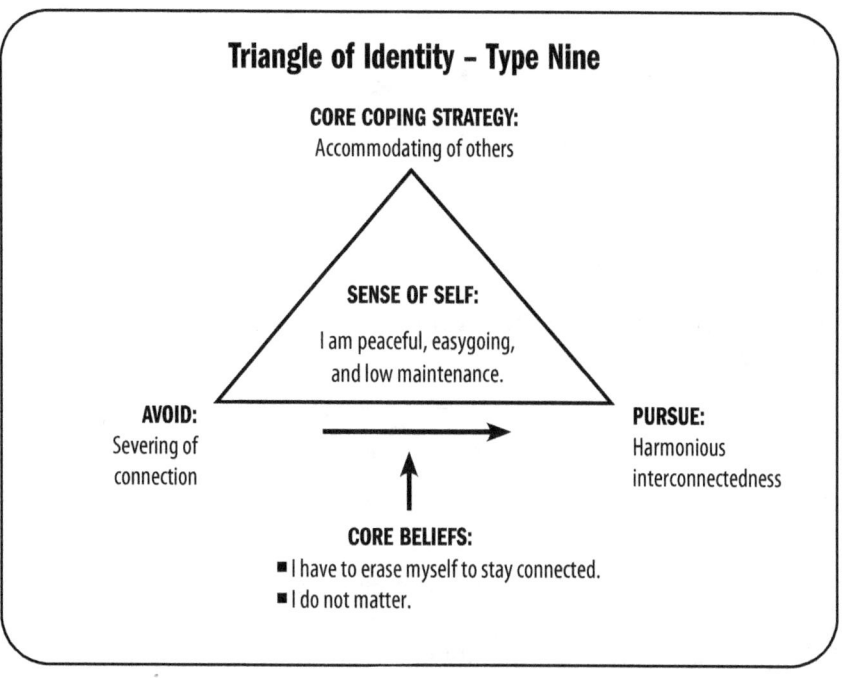

REFLECTION

Do these descriptions resonate with you? If so, how?

_____

_____

_____

If not, do they sound like someone you know?

_____

_____

_____

What questions do you have about this personality type?

_____

_____

_____

What's the main takeaway for you?

_____

_____

_____

THE SOCIAL CLUSTERS

Some people may feel overwhelmed by trying to analyze the nine Enneagram types and determine which one relates to them. One way to help with that process is to cluster the types into groups of three. While there are several approaches for that, I prefer the Social Style Clusters that Riso and Hudson developed after connecting with the work of pioneering psychoanalyst Karen Horney.

Based on Horney's findings, Riso and Hudson discovered that the Enneagram types can be grouped according to how people respond to stress in many social situations, as well as the strategies they use to reduce that anxiety. Looking at the different personality styles from this perspective may help you identify your dominant Enneagram type.

Cluster #1
The Private, Introspective Group

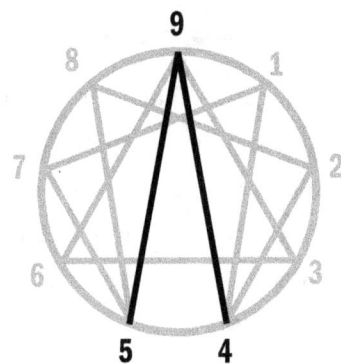

Type 4: The Individualist

Gifts & Healthy Traits: Emotionally intelligent, creative, honest, expressive, engaged.

Sense of Self: I am unique, intuitive, and sensitive.

Type 5: The Investigator

Gifts & Healthy Traits: Curious, focused, insightful, pioneering, self-sufficient.

Sense of Self: I am smart, perceptive, and observant.

Type 9: The Peacemaker

Gifts & Healthy Traits: Receptive, accepting, patient, unpretentious.

Sense of Self: I am calm, peaceful, and easygoing.

The people in this Social Cluster share some common personality structures, including the need for private downtime to process their thoughts and recharge their internal batteries. They may prefer to work independently, and they might be deliberate about carving out sufficient "alone time" before or after interacting with others. Recognizing that need shows wisdom and discernment, and fulfilling it is a positive, healthy approach.

However, this *withdrawing strategy* can become an automatic response when faced with the stress of life and interpersonal relationships. For people in this Social Cluster, they may get into the habit of pulling back from social, physical, emotional, spiritual, or intellectual engagement as a way to cope with uncomfortable situations. Consequently, they find themselves feeling removed and detached.

Cluster #2
The Assured, Confident Group

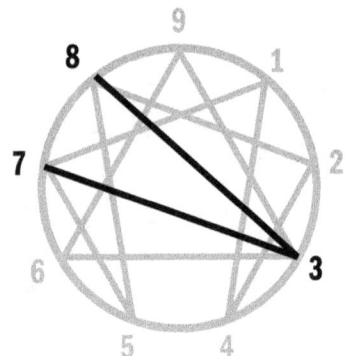

Type 3: The Achiever

    Gifts & Healthy Traits: Goal-oriented, confident, ambitious, flexible, inspiring.

    Sense of Self: I am accomplished and driven with unlimited potential.

Type 7: The Enthusiast

    Gifts & Healthy Traits: Playful, versatile, quick-minded, joyful, entertaining.

    Sense of Self: I am free, spontaneous, fun, and full of life.

Type 8: The Challenger

    Gifts & Healthy Traits: Visionary, assertive, decisive, courageous, charitable.

    Sense of Self: I am strong, in control, and self-reliant.

People who are dominant in this Social Cluster are externally oriented and have expansive energy. They are often powerful, direct communicators who are comfortable being the center of attention. To get things done and make things happen, they employ an *assertive strategy* that allows them to go after what they want while projecting confidence and decisiveness.

When faced with stressful circumstances, these people may automatically rely on that assertive strategy and bulldoze their way through the challenges. They might still get what they want, but it comes at a high cost. They may be perceived by others as pushy or domineering. The desire to exert their power and influence can leave them feeling distanced from other people, as well as themselves.

Cluster #3
The Service-Oriented, Responsible Group

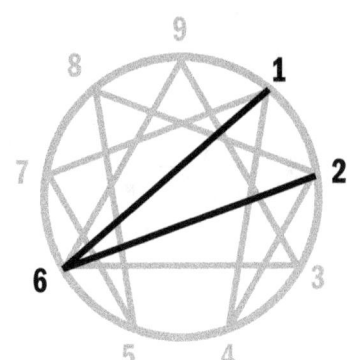

Type 1: The Reformer

    Gifts & Healthy Traits: Principled, purpose-driven, conscientious, wise.

    Sense of Self: I am reasonable, responsible, and objective.

Type 2: The Helper

    Gifts & Healthy Traits: Empathetic, nurturing, openhearted, warm, generous.

    Sense of Self: I am loving, caring, and selfless.

Type 6: The Loyalist

    Gifts & Healthy Traits: Trustworthy, cooperative, committed, open, aware.

    Sense of Self: I am responsible, reliable, and vigilant.

People in this Social Cluster share a strong inner sense of obligation, and they feel a distinct sense of duty to serve others. They are vigilant about following the rules—the ones imposed by others as well as the ones in their own minds. They are proactive about taking responsibility to make things right and caring for the people around them.

When facing stressful situations, their *dutiful strategy* becomes a habitual pattern that heightens their awareness of things that need to be corrected. They feel compelled to do more and more, always staying busy. They begin to experience anxiety and burnout when they feel overly responsible for too many people and commitments. They neglect to take care of their own needs, and they can become resentful when they don't feel appreciated.

THE FINAL POINTS

We'll talk more in Chapter Five about how to accurately determine your Enneagram type, but I want to address a few final details before we move on.

Although the contemporary Enneagram has been around for many decades, it recently experienced a big surge in popularity. Some people today may consider it trendy and toss around the results like it's a party game. I hope you'll remember that the Enneagram is much, much more than that. It's a rich map of the human experience, and it represents a profound field of knowledge that supports stunning transformation.

I encourage you to think of your Enneagram type as the key that can unlock the door to Deep Living. As you increase your awareness of the unique gifts (and limiting patterns) that come with your personality type, you'll be on the road to building a relationship with yourself that's genuine and authentic. You'll have what you need to make sense of much of your life up to now: how and why you made decisions, interacted with others, and handled stress. And going forward, you'll have a wider range of options available with a framework and transformative processes to help you make more effective choices.

Put another way, the brief profiles and the Triangles of Identity presented in this chapter reflect the default ways of "doing life" for each of the nine personalities. Are there one or more profiles that resonate with you? This is generally the easiest way to discover your core type. And once you do, it can be an astonishing experience to see how your particular Enneagram type is expressed through your own life, coming face-to-face with your personality in a different way.

The healthy gifts you most love about your personality will always be available to you. But remember: There's more of you underneath!

What the profiles do *not* reveal is your more authentic nature: the dimension of you that lies beyond your personality. To access your more expansive self, you'll need to dive below the surface of life. That's the purpose of Deep Living: inviting you into your more precious, real, and lovable self.

Up next, we'll discuss how to apply your Enneagram results and move below the surface as part of Deep Living.

CHAPTER FOUR

Integrating the Power of Presence

Once people discover their Enneagram types, they often experience some light-bulb moments when it comes to their habitual patterns:

> "Wow, I do that all the time, but I never stopped to think about why. Now I'm getting some insights!"
> "Well, that explains why I feel uncomfortable in those situations."
> "No wonder I react like that when I get frustrated."
> "I've always felt misunderstood, but now I realize we all experience life from a different perspective."

Without a doubt, the Enneagram offers a powerful lens through which we can see our personalities and habits in unexpected ways. But this framework isn't the end of the story; it's just the beginning.

On the road to building a better relationship with ourselves, think of the Enneagram as the gateway to Deep Living. We can walk through that gate, armed with the information about our personalities. But, from my perspective, the most potent way to experience a meaningful and sustainable difference throughout that journey is by being more present—not only to how I think and act, but to what is happening inside me. When I'm more present to my own experience, I can also become more present to what is actually happening around me. That's the focus of this chapter.

DEEP LIVING THROUGH PRESENCE: THE ESSENTIAL PRINCIPLES

Presence is the single most important component of Deep Living. But it's a word that has been so overused today that its true meaning and significance may be lost. We might hear someone say that the CEO exudes executive presence. We may put away our phones during dinner so we can be present and "in the moment" with our families. The instructor for a professional development course could encourage us to increase our presence and self-awareness if we want to get ahead.

Presence through Deep Living has a different meaning.

In this context, presence is the practice of having a direct experience with our inner selves at any given moment. We recognize the sensations in our bodies, notice what is happening in our hearts, and become aware of our mental activity. We are expanding our ability to notice there is far more going on within us than just our ideas and concepts. With a greater level of presence, we notice that we have more sources of internal feedback available to help us connect with ourselves. The grounded body, open heart, and quiet mind are well-known in the Enneagram field as the three centers of intelligence.

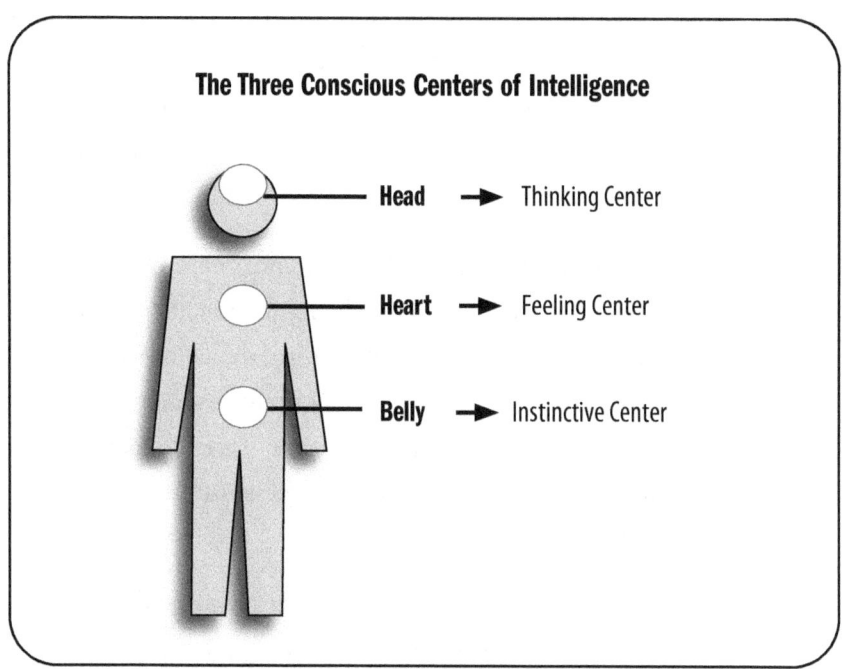

Our heightened awareness of these innate centers provides a surprising pathway to go below the "interference stories" that we tell ourselves about who we are and why things are the way they are. Learning to experience the movement of our breath and the sensations in our bodies brings us into the present moment. When we learn to "be with" what is in our hearts, we not only recognize which feelings are coming up, but also connect with our sense of compassion and kindness for ourselves and others. We begin to notice the space between thoughts and come into contact with greater clarity that is possible within our head center. Most importantly, we can start to trust the new insights that are more easily available to us.

While this may be an entirely different way of relating to your own experience, *it matters*. These centers of intelligence are real sources of information and wisdom. It takes time to develop our connection with them, but as we practice bringing them into our awareness on a regular basis, we can acknowledge them as our own *internal resources*. If you're at all like me, the results may surprise you. I was astonished to realize how much of my own life energy I was ignoring simply because I didn't have the knowledge, the tools, or the support of others to guide me.

Becoming more aware of our centers of intelligence helps us address and release our inner struggles. The practice of being judgment-free builds our capacity to fully accept ourselves as human. In turn, that allows us to loosen the grip of our personalities and enter into an entirely new relationship with ourselves that can involve powerful transformation. It enables our authentic nature to shine through. In truth, this whole process invites us into what I refer to as a *trust walk*.

With so many facets to that definition, let's break it down and look at a few ways our centers of intelligence can support becoming more present.

Embracing Acceptance

Imagine several of your dearest friends are in town, and you've invited them to your apartment for dinner. The day before the event, you begin to think your living room looks a little dark and dreary. You pop over to IKEA and pick up a cute floor lamp. As you prepare for their arrival the next day, you turn on the lamp and suddenly notice the thick layer of dust on the end table. That dust has apparently been there for weeks, but you simply didn't notice it until the light was shining right on it. Now what?

Admittedly, some people are wired to think about it this way: "Who cares? Dusting is not a priority for me. If they have a problem with that, too bad."

For others, the natural inclination would be to grab a soft cloth, a paper towel, or a shirt tail and wipe off that end table before the guests arrive. They've seen the problem, and they want to fix it.

The same thing tends to happen when we analyze the results of our Enneagram types. The unconscious attitudes and lifelong behaviors that have always been a part of us without a second thought are now in the spotlight for further consideration. Sometimes that can lead to embarrassment or self-judgment and, consequently, the urge to "fix" whatever seems wrong.

I encourage you to let go of that message.

Nothing about you needs fixing—you are not broken! You are not inherently faulty or inadequate, and you don't need to approach personal growth based on the fundamental assumption that something is wrong. Your exploration is designed to facilitate understanding, not criticism.

Easier said than done, right? Most people would say this perspective goes against everything they've ever thought about themselves. But it's a powerful and life-changing principle that's at the heart of Deep Living. Acceptance of ourselves and of our life journey is far more powerful than self-judgment in terms of our transformation.

Being fully present brings us into a new, kinder relationship with one of our centers of intelligence—our own heart. It also invites us to begin paying more attention to what our body is trying to tell us. Are you experiencing calmness or tension in your shoulders? Is your breathing slow and steady or rapid and uneven? Do you feel energetic or dragged down by a knot in your stomach? Our bodies can give us plenty of clues about what's happening under the surface, but we have to be intentional about identifying the signs.

With presence, we learn to notice other aspects about ourselves that we haven't seen before—and some of those may be uncomfortable. Even embarrassing. But we can approach these realizations with a calm acceptance rather than feeling like we have to push back and actively change who we are.

Releasing the Patterns

We know from the Enneagram that each of the nine personality types is associated with a particular structure that motivates each person's thoughts, behaviors, and emotions. From our perspective, it's comfortable to "do life" from the confines of that structure. It's familiar. It's what we've always known. The patterns are deeply ingrained.

Given that much of our daily life is habitual, repetitious, and automated, the structure of our personalities becomes the wallpaper in every metaphorical room we enter. It's there whether or not we notice it. Consequently, we may run the risk of allowing those natural habits and patterns to define us. And sometimes, those definitions can be extremely limiting.

> "I worry all the time. That's just who I am. Life makes me anxious."
> "I don't have a bad attitude. I'm just wired to think about what might go wrong. If you want glitter and unicorns, go talk to someone else."
> "I'll admit I'm a drama queen. I can't help it. I've always been passionate and emotional."

You might initially think these realizations could be attributed to having great presence. Ironically, it's the lack of presence that can box us into a narrow definition of who we are. I've seen people fall into this trap many times: There's a high probability of mistakenly associating *presence* with *the experience of a pattern*.

If we live our lives on autopilot—without the benefit of presence—the patterns of our personality take charge and restrict our ability to experience life to the fullest. We inadvertently slip into familiar habits that don't serve us well. As you might recall from Chapter Two, we may end up in the grip of our own personalities.

When the personality is in control, we lose the conscious relationship with our centers of intelligence. But we can choose to take conscious breaths and bring our attention back to what is happening within us. We will notice more choices. We can turn the tables and begin the process of healing and releasing our dependence on the personality patterns that keep us stuck. In doing so, they become less powerful.

Keep in mind that we're not on a mission to *get rid of* our personalities. That is neither possible nor desirable. Our personalities will be with us until the end of our lives, and they are part of who we are. Instead, our intention is to learn how to distinguish between personality patterns that reveal our innate gifts when we are more present and those that get in the way of our true well-being by having a grip on us.

Being present ultimately creates a positive circle. The more present you are, the more you can spot a pesky pattern at work. And the more you release your attachment to the patterns, the more present you become. You might even recognize that some of the Inner Critic messages that have been playing on a loop in your head are simply invalid distractions. At that point, your personality is no longer holding you hostage.

Relaxing Into Yourself

The power of presence can produce transformative change and allow us to become more at home in our own skin. But, as you now know, the approach doesn't involve deliberately working to fix anything about ourselves. From that perspective, Deep Living is rather counterintuitive. So, how does it work?

Using the wisdom of the Enneagram, you can step back and envision a gentle buffer around the personality structure you've discovered. It's like seeing yourself through a wide-angled lens instead of a tight, close-up shot. Creating that space around your personality allows you to objectively yet tenderly recognize the habits and patterns that have become automatic. That realization can spark a more creative train of awareness:

> "Oh, there I go again. It's my usual Enneagram 3 response to make this a competition, even though it's not. I now understand why I do that, and it's okay. But I can also see that this situation doesn't really call for trying to prove I'm the best. There are other options for my response, and I can think about this a different way. What a relief to not feel like I always have to prove myself! I'm also noticing some sort of change within me. I'm not sure exactly what it is, but my heart feels different now."

Can you sense how this process works in stark contrast to actively trying to fix something or make yourself better? Instead of pushing for change, it involves relaxing into yourself—not holding onto your ideas about *who you think you are* so tightly. You may notice that your heart begins to open more as your body releases some of its tension. By letting go of your old habits, you're allowing the space for a broader range of possibilities rather than viewing the world through the tunnel vision you might be used to. It's liberating! And you'll experience a huge sigh of relief when you can go through life without feeling constrained by your own faulty expectations.

When you combine inner knowledge with presence, changes will happen within you. Your personality and its patterns have less control, which leads to a subtle repositioning of the way you approach life. The context of your thinking is altered. Your perspectives shift. You begin to see new alternatives and make different decisions. That's when you are operating on the healthier side of the Enneagram spectrum, no longer trapped inside the boundaries of a false identity.

Through the experience of Deep Living, you'll allow yourself to be fully human and authentic—to align your inner and outer selves in a way that repairs your emotional disconnect and relieves the layers of stress that have been gnawing at you. You'll relax into yourself, and you'll begin to feel at home with who you truly are at your core.

Using the earlier examples, here's what that unconscious shift in thinking might sound like:

WITHOUT PRESENCE *Limited by personality patterns*	WITH PRESENCE *Aware and open to new choices*
"I worry all the time. That's just who I am. Life makes me anxious."	"I've done a lot of worrying in the past, and it just weighs me down. I'll do what I can to create a positive outcome. Then I'll relax and save my mental energy for something else."
"I don't have a bad attitude. I'm just wired to think about what might go wrong. If you want glitter and unicorns, go talk to someone else."	"I do have a knack for identifying the potential pitfalls in new ideas and strategies. I'm a great risk manager, but I should listen before I jump in with my objections. Sometimes there's an upside I don't see, and maybe the risk is worth it."

| **WITHOUT PRESENCE** | **WITH PRESENCE** |
Limited by personality patterns	Aware and open to new choices
"I'll admit I'm a drama queen. I can't help it. I've always been passionate and emotional."	"Being perceived as high maintenance is really working against me—in my career and in on-line dating. If I rein some of that in, life might be less of a struggle."

This points out something quite interesting. Knowing your Enneagram type does more than just tell you *who you are*. When you are present, it also tells you *who you are not*. The more present you are, the less the patterns of personality have a grip on you. That's the core premise of Deep Living.

The inner shifts you experience through this process become translated into changes in your external life. You may not even realize the change has happened, but it has. It's a pervasive paradox that generally leaves people bewildered because it is so far outside the general understanding of how life works.

> *You aren't actively changing anything,*
> *but everything about your life changes.*

Through Deep Living, you can challenge the faulty core beliefs of your Enneagram type and uncover the underlying truths that transcend the patterns of your personality.

ENNEAGRAM	FAULTY CORE BELIEFS	DEEPER TRUTH
TYPE 1 The Reformer	I have to make things right. I can't afford to make a mistake, so I always need to be careful.	I realize it's not my responsibility to fix everything. I can relax and relish the abundant joys in life.
TYPE 2 The Helper	The needs of others must come first.	I ask myself, "What do I need?" and I willingly receive help.
TYPE 3 The Achiever	My worth and my value come from my accomplishments. I want to be perceived as successful.	I am enough without doing anything. How other people see me is none of my business.
TYPE 4 The Individualist	I feel like I'm missing something important. No one understands me.	I am whole. I can be unique and still have beautiful things in common with others.
TYPE 5 The Investigator	I have to figure things out for myself, so I need to gather as much knowledge as possible.	I don't need to know everything. I can participate in life (not just observe) and believe that I'll find the answers when I need them.
TYPE 6 The Loyalist	The world is threatening and dangerous. I can't trust others.	There are good things in the world. I have the courage to explore them, and my security lies within me.
TYPE 7 The Enthusiast	My source of satisfaction comes from outside of me, and I'm constantly in search of that.	My fulfillment exists in experiencing the exquisiteness of the here and now.

ENNEAGRAM	FAULTY CORE BELIEFS	DEEPER TRUTH
TYPE 8 **The Challenger**	I need to be in control and demonstrate my power. I never want to appear weak.	Being vulnerable is the source of my true strength.
TYPE 9 **The Peacemaker**	To stay connected and avoid conflict, I have to fade into the background.	My presence and my opinions matter. My engagement contributes to true peace.

Deep Living has many more layers than can be addressed in this book, but I hope you have gained a glimpse of how this process could measurably impact your own life. There's so much more to you below the surface than you've ever imagined, and Deep Living can help you discover it. You don't have to go through every day feeling disconnected and misunderstood.

The next chapter will describe how you can take the next steps toward building a healthier, more authentic relationship with yourself.

CHAPTER FIVE

Taking the Next Steps

I hope you have been intrigued by the process of Deep Living and the many benefits it can produce in your life. If so, there are several things you can do to expand your knowledge in this area and continue along the journey.

TAP INTO THE SOURCE MATERIAL

As I've mentioned before, this book is designed to be an on-ramp that introduces the essential principles and practices of Deep Living. The primary source material listed below can provide you with a wealth of additional information—including extra layers of knowledge, diverse examples, development suggestions, and more detailed graphics. I hope you'll continue your journey of self-discovery with these helpful books:

- ❖ ***Deep Living with the Enneagram: Recovering Your True Nature*** (Revised/Updated 2020) by Roxanne Howe-Murphy

    This international bestseller features a more comprehensive and nuanced presentation of this subject. The book provides extensive wisdom about using presence to stretch beyond the boundaries of your personality in a way that transforms your relationship with yourself.

❖ ***Guidebook for Deep Living: A Companion to Deep Living with the Enneagram*** (2023) by Moira McCaskill with Laurie Scott Cummins, Roxanne's colleagues at the Deep Living Lab

> This workbook allows you to personalize the Deep Living journey with self-inquiry prompts and exploratory exercises that help you form conscious intentions for developing presence and relaxing personality structures. It can give voice to your inner experience and support you in discovering the thread that runs through your unique and precious life.

Both of these books are available at Amazon.com or many retail booksellers.

Coaches, facilitators, and human development professionals can find information about pertinent resources in the Appendix of this book.

DETERMINE YOUR ENNEAGRAM TYPE

Since the Enneagram is a cornerstone of Deep Living, an obvious next step would be to identify your specific personality type.

An excellent and highly effective way to determine your Enneagram type is with the help of a coach certified in this work. These professionals are trained in the methodology and can personalize the process to suit your specific needs.

I highly recommend the **Deep Living Lab (DeepLivingLab.org)**, which offers one-on-one virtual Enneagram-Typing Discovery Sessions as well as individual coaching, courses, workshops, and retreats. The Lab also enables community members in pursuit of Deep Living to join in professionally facilitated Circles, which are groups that provide collaborative support. Choosing this kind of customized option really is the gold standard for helping you identify your core personality type.

While there are many Enneagram assessments available online, I would like to add a word of caution about the margin of error involved. There's often a discrepancy between *how we want to be seen* and *how we actually function in life*. That's human nature. Unfortunately, that also impacts the way we answer assessment questions.

Sometimes people read the summary of an Enneagram type and immediately believe that's the description of themselves. They get attached to the idea, and it skews the way they respond on the assessment. In addition, some types have commonalities in terms of external expression. But what really distinguishes one personality type from another are the inner motivations that drive their behaviors (things like their core beliefs, Inner Critic messages, and what they avoid). Without the support of a coach to help them be curious and explore more thoroughly, they won't get the benefits of Deep Living that they would with an accurate Enneagram result.

With that said, I recommend starting with the official online assessment from The Enneagram Institute known as the Riso-Hudson Enneagram Type Indicator (RHETI®). Since I was trained in the Riso-Hudson work, this version is my go-to assessment. It has been scientifically validated and provides thought-provoking type summaries. You can access that at www.EnneagramInstitute.com.

Another validated tool is the iEQ9, which is available at www.integrative9.com. It provides a complex range of results that have applications in a variety of settings.

The RHETI and iEQ9 assessments are both highly respected and do require fees. While you may find some free Enneagram tests online, recognize that they may or may not be scientifically validated. I recommend caution in assuming accuracy of their outcomes, but you may want to try a few and see how they compare with one another.

Taking all of those things into account, I've found it can be very helpful to combine the results of a validated Enneagram assessment with a coaching session to further identify and explore your core type.

BEGIN BUILDING YOUR CAPACITY FOR PRESENCE

Another foundational part of Deep Living is becoming more present. This is a lifelong learning process rather than a skill we master. It takes practice and patience, and other resources go into this subject with significantly more depth. However, there are some qualities you can begin to nurture that will help you experience more moments of presence. These include trust, curiosity, honesty, compassion, and courage.

Trust

Getting to know our inner selves can sometimes feel a little intimidating. But we have to enter the process with the fundamental trust that it will be a meaningful experience—that Deep Living will be worth the effort. We also have to believe that what we uncover about ourselves is real and authentic.

If we want to have presence, a foundation of trust makes it possible. Certain points along the journey may be uncomfortable, but trust is what propels us through those moments. Step by step, we'll make progress and build our confidence.

Some people may frame the idea of trust as faith, depending on their spiritual background. A famous quote attributed to Martin Luther King, Jr., really captures this concept:

> ***"Faith is taking the first step even when you don't see the whole staircase."***

In Deep Living, we begin the journey without knowing what the final destination will look like. But we trust that our self-discovery will lead to a more fulfilling relationship with ourselves.

Curiosity

People with a bold sense of curiosity have a true interest in things they don't yet know and a willingness to discover them. On the surface, that sounds simple, but it's tougher than you might think.

Our minds don't like *not knowing*. Given the choice between a known and an unknown, most people will choose the known. And when we don't know something, our natural tendency is to dive in and fill the void with assumptions, theories, and educated guesses. Our thoughts and opinions jump to the front of the line and pretend to be the answers.

Genuine curiosity involves suspending that discomfort with the unknown. It's about taking a deep breath and relaxing, reminding ourselves that we don't need to know everything in advance. Besides, would we really want to know exactly how every day is going to unfold?

When you embrace curiosity, you can approach your life with a more playful attitude, open to a greater range of possibilities. One way to do that is by creating a new habit of starting more sentences with, "I wonder…" or "What if…?"

Consider the person with a core Enneagram Type 6 who has routinely made this comment:

> "It scares me to think about going on a trip to Japan. I don't know anyone, and I don't speak the language. Way too risky to venture out like that on my own."

With a little curiosity, the narrative changes:

> "It scares me to think about going on a trip to Japan. **I wonder** why that feels overwhelming to me. I'm guessing it's because there are so many logistics and opportunities for things to go wrong. I wouldn't feel safe or know what to do, which is understandable. But **what if** I joined a tour group? Someone else would make the arrangements, and I wouldn't be all by myself. It's still out of my comfort zone, but I think I could do that."

Deliberately being curious in the process of building a relationship with ourselves leaves us open to new choices in our lives and new perspectives about our truer nature. Curiosity lightens the experience of self-discovery and reminds us not to take ourselves too seriously.

Best of all, Deep Living helps us bring an open-minded attitude and flexibility to our discoveries, leaving less room for judgment and opinions.

Honesty

Being honest with other people is one thing; being honest with ourselves can be much harder. The truth? We may have spent years (or decades) defining ourselves by the personality structure we perceive to be at the core of who we are. If we uncover contradictory information, it's natural to become a little defensive.

> "That can't be right. I've never thought of myself that way. Must be an error."

To become more present, we have to stop trying to press ourselves into a mold that no longer fits. But we're comfortable with that mold, so it requires radical honesty to realize the mold has become a rut.

When we can bring honesty and sincerity to the process of Deep Living, we become more present and begin to know ourselves on a different level.

Compassion

In the process of recovering our true nature, we get a front-row seat to see the disconnect between the person we've always assumed we are and what's actually underneath. This reality check can be disconcerting and may even evoke an emotional response. It's perfectly normal to feel sadness, grief, embarrassment, or shame. Sometimes there's even intense heartbreak when we realize how much of our lives has been negatively defined and impacted by our personality patterns.

> "I wasted so much time making the same mistake, over and over! Why didn't I recognize this sooner instead of automatically repeating the behavior that caused so much pain for me and for others?"

That's why compassion is another critical quality that enables our ability to experience presence. Along the journey of self-discovery, we all need to pack some grace and a nonjudgmental attitude.

Ideally, we would have understood our personality patterns earlier, but we can't change that. What we *can* change is how we respond to the new information we've uncovered. It's important to compassionately meet ourselves wherever we are, even though the new insights may be painful.

If one of your close friends shared some personal, less-than-positive realizations she discovered about herself, you would likely be supportive. Give yourself that same benefit of the doubt. Avoid the temptation to start labeling certain thoughts or actions as inherently good or bad. Be gentle with yourself, and let compassion take the lead in everything you do.

Courage

Examining the layers below the surface of our usual behavioral and emotional patterns requires a big dose of courage. In fact, this quality is tightly intertwined with the others in this section. It takes courage to trust the process, to be curious, to be honest, and to be compassionate.

One way to build your courage is to find your motivation for getting to know yourself better. Are you trying to alleviate the uncomfortable feelings of the disconnect between your inner and outer self? Are you interested in understanding more about what really drives you? Or are you simply hoping for something better in life? Whatever it is, knowing your motivation will be a strong incentive for the pursuit of Deep Living.

The courage you need is right there, ready to be cultivated and applied.

ADOPT SOME HELPFUL PRACTICES

My clients often understand that developing presence is an ongoing process of learning and development. And yet, they still find themselves craving some concrete strategies for getting started. If that resonates with you, the following suggestions may be helpful as you work to build your capacity for presence and get to know yourself on a deeper level.

Commit to Conscious Breathing

Notice the breath moving in and out of your body and feel the changes that occur through the experience. This level of awareness interrupts the automatic activity of your personality, calms the mind, reduces emotional responses, and gives you access to more of *you*.

Notice Your Sensations

Pay close attention to identify the source of any sensations you are feeling. Are you experiencing tightness in the chest, furrowed brows, tension in your neck and shoulders, a racing pulse, a stomachache, or shallow breathing? How prominent are those sensations? Are they increasing or decreasing? Approach them with a curious and open mind, even if it feels strange. This allows you to practice going below the story that you might be telling yourself about a particular situation and get in touch with how you are affected. There is a hidden intelligence here, and it brings you closer to yourself.

Practice the Art of Silence

Set aside time for meditation or another discipline that quiets your mind and your inner dialogue. As an alternative, just find an environment of solitude that's free from distractions. Especially in the early stages of quieting yourself, it can be difficult to shut out all the internal and external noise so you can get in touch with your inner self. It gets easier! Just keep practicing.

Pay Attention to Your Heart

Block out all the competing signals and focus on your heart, which is the center through which you experience openness, tenderness, receptivity, authenticity, and love without conditions. When you want to increase your presence and know your inner truth, your heart will guide you if you listen deeply and honestly. Without developing your capacity to be in direct contact with your own heart, it is easy to feel lost, lonely, or fearful. Make it a habit to listen and *really hear* what your heart is telling you.

Monitor Your Inner Critic

Recognize the voice of your Inner Critic and remember to discount its negative messages. Call it out and playfully confront it. ("Oh yeah, I heard you. Thanks for that thought, but I don't need any more of your advice. Scram!") Then work to deactivate the impact by bringing your attention back to your heart and showing yourself unconditional acceptance.

Spend Some Time Surrounded by Nature

Breathe in fresh air and marvel at the beauty around you—that's a wonderful way to center yourself on the path to becoming more present. Perhaps you are appreciating the serenity of softly falling snow, watching colorful leaves from a giant oak tree dance toward the ground, or delighting in the fairy-like wings of a hummingbird drinking nectar from a flower. Allow time to be with yourself outdoors, and let the wonders of nature refresh your soul.

MAKE A COMMITMENT

Taking the next steps on the path toward Deep Living will help you continue your momentum. Make the commitment to do this for yourself. There's so much more of you to uncover beneath your personality, and you are worth the effort! I hope the options I've described can help you move forward with greater confidence as you build a more meaningful relationship with the most important person in your life: *YOU*.

Conclusion

The journey of self-discovery has played such a pivotal role in my life, and I am grateful every day for the gifts that emerge through Deep Living. With that said, articulating the exact change that occurs on the inside through this process isn't easy. It's like the switch from living in a flat, black-and-white existence to seeing yourself (and the world) in the vivid colors of 3D IMAX. There's really no comparison.

The problem is, many people don't know there is an alternative. They put one foot in front of the other each day, slogging through their familiar lives without any idea there's something more out there. They assume the underlying feelings of disconnection and struggle are a normal part of life.

I hope the pages of this book have compelled you to learn more about Deep Living and to pursue the brilliant, colorful layers of your life that are now within your reach. There *is* something more. If you've been weighed down by an inescapable sense of dissatisfaction, Deep Living could be the ray of hope you've been searching for to boost your well-being.

As you ponder the possibilities, think about Deep Living as a lifelong adventure with limitless rewards. Through presence, every moment of your life can provide an amazing opportunity to experience something new about yourself. It all starts with staying more aware and connecting with the person you are at your core.

You *can* develop the capacity to experience a new relationship with yourself, and I want to encourage you to take the first step with inquisitiveness and empathy. Remember that it's a journey with no deadline or final destination. Even today, I'm still discovering new things about myself as I focus on being more aware in the present moment. It's an ongoing intention of noticing and releasing unnecessary inner noise and external distractions. And when I do that, it opens me up to being more appreciative of the wonders that are part of life.

As we wrap up, I want to share a story with you about a woman who experienced the life-changing impact of Deep Living.

DEEP LIVING IN ACTION

Jade was a university faculty member in Health and Human Services, and her mission was to design quality wellness systems for underserved communities. She was extremely dedicated, and she had high standards for herself, her students, and even her colleagues. But something was not working in her life.

Jade frequently felt anxious or irritable. It seemed like things never went her way, at home and at work. She developed clear, targeted strategies for team projects, but then she harbored quite a bit of resentment when coworkers didn't pull their weight or just wanted to cut corners. She also began to sense that some people in the department were avoiding her, and she wondered why they weren't interested in collaborating. Every day felt like an uphill battle.

CONCLUSION

All of those underlying feelings were taking a toll, and Jade started suffering with bouts of depression. She described it as going down a "rabbit hole" of darkness, followed by desperately trying to find a way to pull herself back out again so she could function.

Unfortunately, crawling out of the rabbit hole didn't usually last for very long. The relief was short-lived, and then she found herself sliding right back down into the darkness. Jade had resigned herself to this distressing way of life, thinking these uncomfortable feelings were just normal for her.

One weekend, Jade had lunch with her sister Kelly. Among their many conversations, Kelly mentioned a book she was reading called *Deep Living with the Enneagram*. Jade had heard of the Enneagram and thought it sounded interesting, but she never had the time to investigate it. She had questions! Kelly explained that she worked with a coach at the Deep Living Lab to jumpstart the process and felt like it had really changed her perspective. Jade decided it was worth exploring.

She picked up a copy of the book and connected with a professional at the Deep Living Lab who helped her identify that she was an Enneagram Type 1. Jade was fascinated to discover that everyone has an Inner Critic, but people with her dominant personality type tend to have one that's much louder than others. That realization stopped her in her tracks.

Upon reflection, she could see how her Inner Critic had derailed so many things in her life, spewing criticism and contempt at every turn. Existing with the constant stream of internal negativity felt like a "life sentence" to Jade. She lived with it for so long and assumed there was nothing she could do about it. *That's just the way it is for me*, she thought.

Through working with the Deep Living books and increasing her presence, she recognized how hard she had been on herself for decades. It was classic Enneagram Type 1 behavior. She was often tense and felt rigid. Many times, that discomfort spilled over to being critical of the people around her. Jade's constant, underlying irritability was silently infecting her relationships with family, friends, and coworkers.

The biggest shock? Her entire career was focused on championing the causes of health and wellness, but she wasn't even prioritizing those things in her own life. The irony was tragic.

Deep Living was a huge wake-up call for Jade. In this work, she saw a glimmer of hope for a different way of life. A light bulb was turning on for her. She started to envision a future in which the volume of her Inner Critic was turned to a much lower level.

Jade began to take well-being and self-compassion seriously, appreciating herself as a fully authentic human with gifts and imperfections that are all part of the package and privilege of being alive. With the support of her Deep Living coach, she learned some practices that helped her relax her body, attend to her heart, and let go of the condescending messages that kept replaying in her head.

The much-needed process of getting to know herself better was somewhat bittersweet. She experienced extraordinary grief when she realized how much of her life had been spent trapped by unconscious personality patterns. Those patterns had left a damaging imprint on the personal and professional parts of her world. If only she had known, she could have saved herself from immeasurable pain. Over and over again, she asked herself: *Why doesn't everyone learn about this earlier in life?*

On the positive side, one of the greatest gifts of Deep Living for Jade was experiencing more moments of lightness and real joy. She had forgotten what those were like and, honestly, doubted she would ever feel them again. They were so uplifting! Refreshing. Liberating. Learning to like and accept herself for exactly who she was changed everything.

Jade committed to continue her healthier, life-affirming journey. She noticed substantially less interference from her Inner Critic, her stress level was greatly diminished, and her well-being increased in dramatic ways. She was able to interrupt the old pattern of hyperfocusing on what wasn't working the way she thought it should. She was also able to look at situations and decisions from a new perspective, visualizing options and responses beyond her typical comfort zone. Her colleagues and students even noticed the shift. Jade's relationships with them improved, and her interactions with them were much more positive.

Through her transformation with Deep Living, Jade was increasingly effective at developing and implementing the wellness systems she had long ago envisioned for the underserved neighborhoods in her state. She radiated an authentic inner joy in working toward this career goal, and her coworkers were excited to support her. By getting to know herself on a deeper level, she was able to make stronger connections with the people around her and see a future with bright potential.

Naturally, Jade still faces a range of challenges in her life today, but being grounded in the principles of Deep Living gives her new ways to overcome the roadblocks. Her attitude and her outlook have been transformed by the unexpected insights she discovered. And yes, her world really does seem to be moving from black and white to a kaleidoscope of colors. Jade would be the first to tell you that Deep Living has changed her life, and she continues to make it a priority every single day.

STAYING THE COURSE

No matter what Enneagram type you are, the same kind of transformation is possible for you.

If you've been existing on the surface of your life, I invite you to explore the opportunities for change through Deep Living. There's a heartfelt contentment that comes from aligning your inner and outer worlds—from knowing what's underneath your personality and being comfortable in your own skin.

I genuinely want that for you.

It's my sincerest wish that reading this book has sparked your curiosity, renewed your courage, ignited your compassion for yourself, and deeply nourished your soul.

Here's to you—and the real, uplifting sense of beauty and well-being that are possible for your life.

APPENDIX

For Coaches & Human Development Professionals

If you are a coach or facilitator involved with a transformational practice, you've probably already recognized the value that the principles of Deep Living could offer your clients. I know firsthand the enormous impact this approach had on my work as a professional coach, so I felt compelled to include this bonus section specifically for you.

As the concept of Deep Living began to emerge for me, I recognized in hindsight that my early years of coaching efforts may have fallen short in helping clients get to the heart of the matter as I worked with them on issues they found challenging. Once I integrated the principles of a presence-based approach to the Enneagram into my coaching sessions, I was astonished by the accelerated breakthroughs my clients experienced.

I had the privilege of sharing the remarkable results of this approach with other coaches and professional practitioners through my first book in 2007, ***Deep Coaching: Using the Enneagram as a Catalyst for Profound Change***.

(A second edition with 40% new material was published in 2022.) Writing this book helped me to crystallize the principles of Deep Living and completely altered the way I coach my clients. I believe it can do the same for you.

Within *Deep Coaching*, you'll find a comprehensive and more nuanced approach to this topic, with expanded information on the nine Enneagram types, transformational processes, exercises, and helpful coaching tips. The book provides specific guidance on how to use Enneagram types as a powerful starting place for supporting your clients in their transformative movement toward wholeness. You'll also learn strategies that enable you to coach from a novel perspective and adopt a radically gracious approach to the change process for your clients.

To give you a glimpse of the essential principles I've taught to professionals over many years, I'd like to share with you the Five Pillars that form the foundation of the Deep Living approach to coaching and facilitation—what I call Deep Coaching.

FIRST PILLAR
THE ENNEAGRAM

The Enneagram is a valuable map for understanding the full range of the human condition, and it shows people how their personalities can naturally reinforce their default reactions. As coaches, we typically work with clients who are experiencing some obstacles to growth and development that are based in the personality structure itself. It is not uncommon for us humans to attribute unsatisfying experiences to external factors. For example, we might blame our problems on a terrible boss, disruptive children, or a difficult childhood.

Once our clients land on a core Enneagram type and have the benefit of our nonjudgmental support, we can help them recognize the influence of their personality types on their struggles. This is not from the perspective of self-blame, but from an honest intention to gain awareness of how they show up in life when living from the automatic frame of reference linked to their dominant personality type.

By bringing attention to what lies below the level of behavior through Deep Living, we as coaches can enable our clients to identify some type-related motivators involved in their choices: assumptions and biases, projections, default emotional drives and fixations, and strategies for coping. The recognition of unconscious motivators can serve as a pivotal accelerator in the clients' healing of their inner disconnects and the development of their capacity to identify new alternatives for their actions.

From another angle, coaches also have the privilege of helping clients recognize the blessings that are inherent in every Enneagram type. Those who associate with a certain type tend to have a unique set of gifts and qualities that can be used in positive ways to benefit the people around them. That's why I often call the Enneagram a map of love. These precious gifts are greatly needed in today's environment of fractured communities, hurting families, and a disconnected world. By nurturing our clients as they lean into their strengths, we can support them as they thrive and grow.

SECOND PILLAR
THE CATALYST OF PRESENCE

Coaching that uses the Deep Living framework is based on the ability to be genuinely present, which applies to our clients and to us as professionals. When we are in direct contact with our three innate centers of intelligence (a grounded body, an open heart, and a clear head), we have an inner structure that allows us to be more present with our clients. These same centers are also vitally important for our clients, as they seek to be present, right here and now.

Presence is the catalyst that leads to successful coaching outcomes. When both parties are more fully present in the coaching relationship, clients have a greater capacity to respond with open curiosity and kindness to current circumstances, to make decisions that are aligned with their deeper guidance, and to take effective next steps.

A fundamental orientation to presence applies to all life circumstances: facing difficulties in relationships, developing an authentic sense of self, rehabilitating after an injury, living with a serious illness, working in organizations with ineffective dynamics, shifting to a new career path, challenging a social injustice, or diving deeper into one's spiritual path.

THIRD PILLAR
THE COUNTERINTUITIVE CHANGE PROCESS

The Deep Living approach runs completely counter to the traditional, linear, goal-oriented style of coaching. Rather than entering conversations with a preconceived idea of what the coaching outcome should look like, we meet our clients where they are and without judgment. The process is informed by presence, which makes it inherently open, reflective, and receptive as it supports greater access to both the client's and the coach's deeper dimensions of intelligence.

While it may seem paradoxical, this approach is instrumental in helping clients develop a deeper relationship with themselves that lies beyond their personality's usual ways of coping.

FOURTH PILLAR
THE INNATE NATURE

The human experience is often permeated by a sense of aloneness and separation. When people are wrapped up in the inner bubble of their personalities, they naturally feel disconnected. For some, this sense of separateness may be vague and less conscious. For others, it is undeniably obvious. Either way, the feelings of separation are a delusion of the small, default-based self.

As coaches who apply the principles of Deep Living, we get the opportunity to orient our clients toward interconnectedness, love, and self-acceptance—in other words, discovering the innate nature that's underneath their personalities. The more deeply we come to understand ourselves, the more likely we are to perceive ourselves and others more accurately. With understanding comes a deep admiration for the human condition that we all share. Our hearts become more open and available.

As our clients begin to loosen the grip of the personality and embrace their innate nature, they begin to recognize that they are not as alone and separate as they once thought.

FIFTH PILLAR
THE INNER WORK OF THE COACH

The power of Deep Living to generate transformative change in our clients is dependent on our own applications of these principles as coaches. Our inner work to become more self-aware and oriented toward our spaciousness is a mandatory prerequisite for successfully guiding others through the process.

When we engage in our own quest for growth and well-being by doing deeper work, we support not only our own unfolding but also that of our clients.

Sometimes we may not even be aware of that ripple effect, but it exists. The most effective way to serve our clients is by tapping into the power of Deep Living ourselves.

By integrating these Five Pillars, we can elevate the impact of our coaching in a way that leads to outcomes we couldn't have predicted and our clients never expected. The results can still take my breath away. What a gift it is to walk with others through tender territory and into a new experience of life they never imagined. The added benefit? Witnessing that transformation changes us as well.

Note: A more extensive description of these foundational components can be found in the *Deep Coaching* book.

Selected Bibliography

Almaas, A. H. (2008). *The Unfolding Now: Realizing your true nature through the practice of presence.* Boston: Shambhala Publications.

Arrien, Angeles (2013). *Living in Gratitude: Mastering the art of giving thanks every day.* Boulder, CO: Sounds True.

Brown, Byron (1999). *Soul Without Shame: A guide to liberating yourself from the judge within.* Boston: Shambhala Publications.

Brown, Molly, ed. *Deep Times: A journal of the work that reconnects.* https://journal.workthatreconnects.org/.

Chodron, Pema (2002). *The Places That Scare You: A guide to fearlessness in difficult times.* Boston: Shambhala Publications.

Chryssavgis, John (2008: revised edition). *In the Heart of the Desert: The spirituality of the Desert Fathers and Mothers.* Bloomington, IN: World Wisdom.

Goleman, Daniel (1995). *Emotional Intelligence: Why it can matter more than IQ.* New York: Bantam Books.

Gore, Belinda (forthcoming). *Finding Freedom: Understanding our relationships using object relations and the Enneagram.*

Houston, Jean (1987). *The Search for the Beloved: Journeys in mythology and sacred psychology.* Los Angeles: Jeremy Tarcher.

Howe-Murphy, Roxanne (2022: 2nd edition). *Deep Coaching: Using the Enneagram as a catalyst for profound change.* Santa Fe, NM: Enneagram Press.

Howe-Murphy, Roxanne (2020: revised edition). *Deep Living with the Enneagram: Recovering your true nature.* Santa Fe, NM: Enneagram Press.

Kornfield, Jack (1993). *A Path with Heart: A guide through the perils and promises of spiritual life.* New York: Bantam Books.

Menakem, Resmaa (2017). *My Grandmother's Hands: Racialized trauma and the pathway to mending our hearts and bodies.* Las Vegas: Central Recovery Press.

Nhat Hanh, Thich (April 23, 2014). "Practising Listening with Empathy," Buddhism Now. https://buddhismnow.com/2014/04/23/practising-listening-with-empathy-by-thich-nhat-hanh/.

Palmer, Parker J. (1998). *The Courage to Teach: Exploring the inner landscape of a teacher's life.* San Francisco: Jossey-Bass.

Pransky, Jillian (2017). *Deep Listening: A healing practice to calm your body, clear your mind, and open your heart.* Emeryville, CA: Crown Publishing Group.

Rilke, Rainier Maria (1984). *Letters to a Young Poet.* New York: Random House. (Transcribed by Stephen Mitchell. Original work published after the author's death in 1926.)

Riso, Don Richard, and Russ Hudson (2003: revised edition). *Discovering Your Personality Type: The essential introduction to the Enneagram.* Boston: Houghton Mifflin.

Riso, Don Richard, and Russ Hudson (2000). *Understanding the Enneagram: The practical guide to personality types.* Boston: Houghton Mifflin.

Riso, Don Richard, and Russ Hudson (1999). *The Wisdom of the Enneagram: The complete guide to psychological and spiritual growth for the nine personality types.* New York: Bantam Books.

Salzberg, Sharon (1997). *Lovingkindness: The revolutionary art of happiness.* Boston: Shambhala Publications.

Sardello, Robert (2008). *Silence: The mystery of wholeness.* Berkeley, CA: Goldenstone Press.

About the Author

Roxanne Howe-Murphy

As the creator of the Deep Living principles, Roxanne Howe-Murphy is considered a master teacher, thought leader, and a catalyst for change. She is also a pioneer and global expert in integrating the Enneagram with executive and life coaching. Her groundbreaking book, *Deep Coaching: Using the Enneagram as a Catalyst for Profound Change*, is used regularly by both professionals and laypeople around the world.

Roxanne has spent more than four decades working in diverse fields, including rehabilitation, higher education, coach training, and retreat facilitation. She has also personally done extensive inner work that complements her rich experience to give her a unique area of expertise. Through the years, she has been invited to lead numerous international retreats, and she has had the honor of guiding people from around the world through the process of building better relationships with themselves.

In addition to being a #1 International Best-Selling Author on Amazon, Roxanne is the founder of the Deep Living Lab and the Deep Coaching Institute. She is a former faculty member at San José State University and

Boston University. She is also an accredited teacher with the International Enneagram Association and a certified teacher with The Enneagram Institute of New York.

Roxanne earned an Educational Doctorate degree in Learning and Instruction with a Counseling Psychology emphasis from the University of San Francisco. She holds a Master's degree in therapeutic recreation from San José State University as well as a Bachelor's degree in social work and sociology from the University of Iowa.

Writing is something Roxanne considers to be one of her spiritual practices. Through the process of listening inwardly and allowing words to reach the printed page, she finds that her own awareness deepens and expands. Her books have been translated into Korean and Taiwanese, and her writings have received wide acclaim.

Deep Living with the Enneagram: Recovering Your True Nature has been recognized with multiple awards in Mind/Body/Spirit and Personal Growth literature. These honors include:

- ❖ Winner of the 2020 National Indie Excellence Award (Personal Growth)
- ❖ Silver Medal Winner of the Benjamin Franklin Publisher Award from the Independent Book Publishers Association (Mind/Body/Spirit)
- ❖ Finalist for the 2020 Next Generation Indie Book Award (Mind/Body/Spirit)

ABOUT THE AUTHOR

After living near the ocean for most of her adult life, Roxanne and her husband made the move to Santa Fe, New Mexico, where they savor hiking in the mountains and participating in the vast array of local festivals, multicultural art and music events, and educational activities.

Roxanne is an avid animal lover, which led her to enter the world of animal communication, which she finds both astonishing and humbling. She seldom turns down a decaf (yes, decaf!) frothy cappuccino, a nibble of 88% chocolate, or listening to adventurous new music performed by extraordinary classical musicians on Saturday mornings.

RoxanneHoweMurphy.com

Additional Resources

BOOKS

The following books by Roxanne Howe-Murphy are available on Amazon.com and through many local retailers:

- ❖ ***Deep Living with the Enneagram: Recovering Your True Nature*** (Revised & Updated, 2020)
- ❖ ***Deep Coaching: Using the Enneagram as a Catalyst for Profound Change*** (1st Edition, 2007)
- ❖ ***Deep Coaching: Using the Enneagram as a Catalyst for Profound Change*** (2nd Edition with 40% new information, 2022)

Please contact the publisher for information about bulk discounts.

The following workbook was authored by Roxanne's colleagues at the Deep Living Lab, Moira McCaskill with Laurie Scott Cummins, and is available on Amazon.com:

- ❖ ***Guidebook for Deep Living: A Companion to Deep Living with the Enneagram*** (new publication, 2023)

Please contact the Deep Living Lab for information about bulk discounts.

RETREATS & CUSTOMIZED SUPPORT

The Deep Living Lab is a nonprofit with the mission of contributing to high levels of collective well-being. Through its distinct approach, it delivers guided experiences in building capacities for engaged presence. The team at the Lab offers a wide range of services including Enneagram-Typing Discovery Sessions, coaching, courses, and retreats. In addition, the Lab facilitates small groups called Deep Living Circles, which provide collaborative support for those engaged in moving toward Deep Living. Find out more at DeepLivingLab.com or send a message to info@DeepLivingLab.org.

SUPPLEMENTAL STUDY OPPORTUNITY

EnneaCrossings™ is a related framework and body of knowledge developed by Roxanne in conjunction with her colleague Diana Redmond. Rooted in the principles of Deep Living, it integrates two powerful, ancient symbols: the Enneagram and the intercultural cross, both of which reflect individual and collective spiritual journeys that contribute to our engaged presence in the world. To learn more about this emerging body of work, visit DeepLivingLab.org and watch for Roxanne's upcoming book that addresses this work.

Contact Information

ROXANNE HOWE-MURPHY

info@roxannehowemurphy.com

www.RoxanneHoweMurphy.com

DEEP LIVING LAB

info@DeepLivingLab.org

DeepLivingLab.org

If you pursue the journey of Deep Living and have a wonderful story to tell about the results, I hope you will reach out and share it with me (info@roxannehowemurphy.com). Your comments might be included in a future book, blog post, or promotion—with your permission, of course!

www.ingramcontent.com/pod-product-compliance
Lightning Source LLC
Chambersburg PA
CBHW072050290426
44110CB00014B/1624